CHAPTER 1 THE MULTI-STORE MODEL

Specification: The multi-store model of memory: sensory register, short-term memory and long-term memory. Features of each store: coding, capacity and duration.

What you need to know

Outline Atkinson & Shiffrin's (1968) multi-store model of memory

Outline and evaluate the key features of the model, including the sensory register, short-term memory and long-term memory store, in relation to:

- Coding
- Capacity
- Duration

Evaluate the multi-store model of memory

Multi-Store Model

Atkinson & Shiffrin (1968) proposed one of the earliest models of memory – **the Multi-Store Model (MSM)**. They suggested that memory is made up of three components: **sensory register (SR), short-term memory (STM)** and **long-term memory (LTM)**. According to the model, memories are formed sequentially, and information passes from one component to the next, in a linear fashion.

Each of the three components has a specific type of coding, capacity and duration. **Coding** refers to how information is changed and stored in memory. **Duration** refers to the length of time that information is held in the memory store and capacity refers to the amount of information that can be stored.

Information enters the sensory register via our senses. Our sensory register has an unknown (but supposedly unlimited) capacity and a very limited duration of less than one second (approximately 250 milliseconds). As information enters from all five senses the coding is modality-specific and said to be raw, or unprocessed, information.

Information that is attended to is passed to STM, which has a limited capacity of 7+/-2 'chunks' of information and a limited duration of approximately 20 seconds. Information in our STM is coded in an acoustic format. For example, if you were trying to remember a phone number, you might repeat the number over and over in your head.

Thereafter, rehearsed information is transferred to LTM, which has an unlimited capacity and a lifetime duration. Information in LTM is coded semantically (by meaning) and can be retrieved from LTM to STM when required.

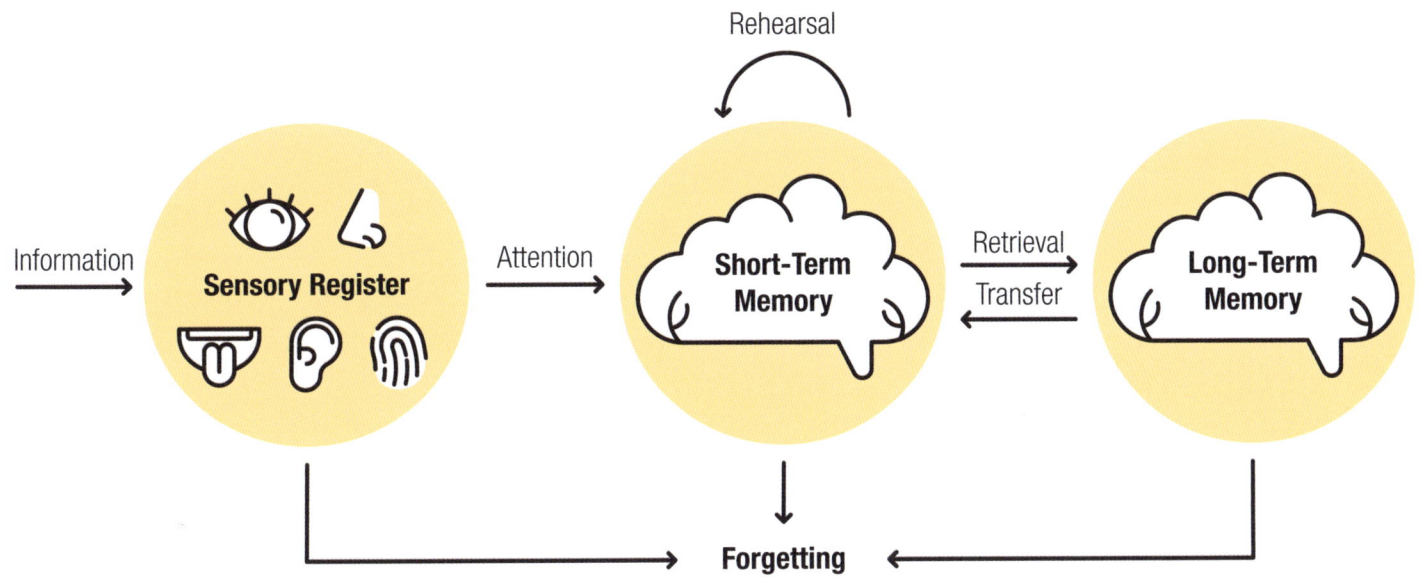

	Sensory Register	Short-Term Memory	Long-Term Memory
Capacity	Unknown, but very large	Limited (7+/-2 'chunks' of information) Jacobs (1887) Miller (1956)	Unlimited
Duration	Very limited (approximately 250 ms)	Limited (20 seconds) Peterson & Peterson (1959)	Lifetime/Years Bahrick (1975)
Coding	Raw/unprocessed information (from ALL 5 senses)	Acoustic (Sound) Baddeley (1966)	Semantic (Meaning) Baddeley (1966)

Research Investigating the MSM

The MSM of memory has been investigated extensively, and research has provided support for the different components of the model. For example, research by Miller (1956) supports the idea that our STM has a capacity of 7+/-2 'chunks' of information; Baddeley (1966) supports the notion of different types of encoding in STM and LTM; Peterson & Peterson (1959) support the idea of a limited duration in STM and Bahrick (1975) supports the idea of an unlimited duration in LTM.

Research: Miller (1956) The Capacity of STM

Aim: To investigate the capacity of STM.

Method: Literature review of published investigations into perception and STM, from the 1930s to 1950s.

Results: This existing research suggested that organising stimulus input into a series of chunks enabled STM to cope with about seven 'chunks', and this was why more than seven digits, words or even musical notes could be remembered successfully. When we try to remember a phone number, which has 11 digits, we chunk the information into groups, for example, 0767…819…45…34, so we only need to remember four chunks of information and not 11 individual digits.

Conclusion: Organisation (or 'encoding') can extend the capacity of STM and enable more information to be stored there, albeit briefly.

Criticisms:

- Miller's (1956) theory is supported by psychological research. For example, Jacobs (1887) conducted an experiment using a digit span test, to examine the capacity of STM for numbers and letters. Jacobs used a sample of 443 female students (aged from 8–19) from the North London Collegiate School. Participants had to repeat back a string of numbers or letters in the same order and the number of digits/letters was gradually increased until the participants could no longer recall the sequence. Jacobs found that the students had an average span of 7.3 letters and 9.3 words, which supports Miller's notion of 7+/-2.

- Although Miller's (1956) theory is supported by psychological research, he did not specify how large each 'chunk' of information could be and therefore we are unable to conclude the exact capacity of STM. Consequently, further research is required to determine the size of information 'chunks' to understand the exact capacity of STM.

Research: Peterson & Peterson (1959) The Duration of STM

Aim: To investigate how different short intervals containing an interference task affect the recall of items presented verbally, and to infer the duration of STM.

Method: The participants were 24 male and female university students. The verbal items tested for recall were 48 three-consonant nonsense syllables (such as JBW or PDX) spelled out letter by letter. These have since been named 'trigrams'. There were also cards containing three-digit numbers (such as 360 or 294).

The researcher spelled the syllable out and then immediately said a three-digit number. The participant had to count down backwards in either 3s or 4s (as instructed) from that number. This was to prevent repetition of the trigram by the participant. At the end of a pre-set interval of between 3 and 18 seconds, a red light went on and the participant had to recall the trigram.

Results: Peterson & Peterson found that the longer the interval the less accurate the recall. At 3 seconds, around 80% of the trigrams were correctly recalled, whereas at 18 seconds only 10% were correctly recalled.

Conclusion: STM has a limited duration of approximately 18 seconds. Furthermore, if we are unable to rehearse information it will not be passed to LTM, providing further support for the MSM and the idea of discrete components.

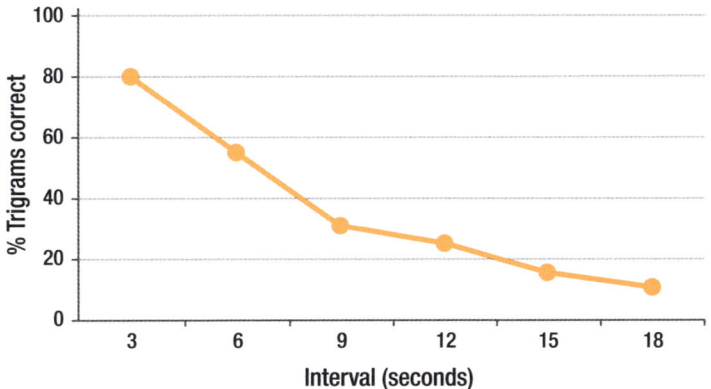

Experiment 1 Relationship between the length of the interval between presentation and recall of the trigrams, and the mean percentage of trigrams recalled correctly

Criticisms:

- Peterson & Peterson used a sample of 24 psychology students, which is an issue for two reasons. Firstly, the psychology students may have encountered the MSM of memory previously and therefore may have demonstrated demand characteristics by changing their behaviour to assist the experimenter. Secondly, the memory of psychology students may be different from that of other people, especially if they had previously studied strategies for memory improvement. As a result we are unable to generalise the results of this study to non-psychology students.

- Furthermore, it could be argued that Peterson & Peterson's study has low levels of ecological validity. In this study participants were asked to recall three-letter trigrams, which is unlike anything people would want to memorise in their everyday lives. As a result we are unable to apply these results to everyday examples of memory and are unable to conclude if the duration of STM may be longer for more important information, such as a vital phone number.

Research: Bahrick (1975) The Duration of LTM

Aim: To investigate the duration of LTM.

Method: 392 American university graduates were shown photographs from their high school yearbook and for each photograph participants were given a group of names and asked to select the name that matched the photographs.

Results: 90% of the participants were able to correctly match the names and faces 14 years after graduating and 60% of the participants were able to correctly match the names and faces 47 years after graduation.

Conclusion: Bahrick concluded that people could remember certain types of information, such as names and faces, for almost a lifetime. These results support the MSM and the idea that our LTM has a lifetime duration (at least 47 years) and is semantically encoded.

Criticisms:

- Bahrick's research used a sample of 392 American university graduates and therefore lacks population validity. Psychologists are unable to generalise the results of Bahrick's research to other populations, for example, students from the UK or Europe. As a result, we are unable to conclude whether other populations would demonstrate the same ability to recall names and faces after 47 years.

- Furthermore, Bahrick found that the accuracy of LTM was 90% after 14 years and 60% after 47 years. His research is unable to explain whether LTM becomes less accurate over time because of a limited duration, or whether LTM simply gets worse with age. This is important because psychologists are unable to determine whether our LTM has an unlimited duration (like the MSM suggests), which is affected by other factors such as getting old, or whether our LTM has a limited duration.

Evaluating the Multi-store Model of Memory

- One strength of the MSM is that there is research to support it. For example, the case of Clive Wearing, who contracted a virus that caused severe amnesia (memory loss). Following the virus, Wearing could only remember information for 20-30 seconds; however, he was able to recall information from his past, for example, his wife's name. Wearing was unable to transfer information from his STM to his LTM but was able to retrieve information successfully. Wearing's case supports the idea that memories are formed by passing information from one store to the next in a linear fashion and that damage to any part of the MSM can cause memory impairment.

- Further support for the MSM comes from psychological studies. For example, Miller (1959) supports the idea of a limited capacity of 7+/-2 chunks of information in STM; Peterson & Peterson (1959) support the idea of a limited duration in STM, of approximately 20 seconds and Bahrick (1975) supports the idea of a lifetime duration in LTM. All these studies support the different elements of the MSM and therefore suggest that the model is an accurate representation of human memory.

- One strength is that there is objective, biological evidence to support the MSM. For example, brain scans have shown that different areas of the brain are active when performing STM tasks (hippocampus) and LTM tasks (motor cortex). The hippocampus is also involved in transferring short-term memories into long-term memories. This suggests that different brain regions are responsible for the different components of the MSM, supporting the idea that our memory is made up of discrete stores.

- One limitation of the MSM is that it is not as sophisticated or in-depth as the Working Memory Model. Whilst the MSM claims STM and LTM to be unitary, the WMM recognises different areas within STM, such as the phonological loop and the visual-spatial sketchpad. This suggests that the MSM may not quite represent the complexity of human memory.

Extension Evaluation: Issues and Debates

- One limitation is that the MSM takes a nomothetic approach to researching memory, trying to create a universal model to explain the process of human memory. An idiographic, individual approach that uses examples of real-life memory may result in a more complex (and arguably more accurate) picture of memory.

- One limitation of the research that supports the MSM is the pattern of experimental reductionism. This is because the research attempts to explain a complex behaviour by relying on isolated variables operationalised in laboratory experiments (e.g. the capacity of STM or the duration of STM). However, as memory is a complex phenomenon, many psychologists argue that reducing memory to isolated variables undermines the complexity of human memory.

POSSIBLE EXAM QUESTIONS

1 Define what is meant by the term 'coding'? (2 marks)

2 Define what is meant by the term 'capacity'? (2 marks)

3 Define what is meant by the term 'duration'? (2 marks)

Exam Hint While students are often able to define these key terms accurately, many students fail to pick up a second mark as they struggle with the elaboration of their definitions. An easy way to ensure that students secure the full marks is to provide an example related to the sensory register, STM or LTM. For example, coding refers to how information is changed and stored in memory. Information in STM is coded in an acoustic format.

4 Describe how psychologists have investigated the duration of STM. (4 marks)

Exam Hint The key word to note in this question is 'how'. Students are expected to describe how researchers have conducted their research – the method – in detail. Therefore, students might outline the method of Peterson & Peterson by explaining what the participants were required to do and how duration was measured in this study.

5 Complete the following table, adding the missing information (A, B, C and D) in relation to the features of the multi-store model. (4 marks)

	Sensory Register	Short-Term Memory	Long-Term Memory
Capacity	A	7 +/- 2	Unlimited
Duration	B	C	Lifetime
Coding	Raw (Unprocessed) / Modality Specific	Acoustic	D

6 Outline two differences between the STM and LTM. (4 marks)

 **Exam Hint** Your answer should focus on the differences between the two memory stores, rather than merely describe traits of STM and LTM.

7 According to Atkinson and Shiffrin, the STM and LTM are very different. Outline how research has demonstrated the difference between STM and LTM. (4 marks)

 **Exam Hint** For this question, students need to link the research (e.g. Peterson & Peterson and Bahrick) to the question and say how the results from these two studies show that the STM and LTM are different.

8 Laura still uses an old-fashioned phone book and wants to phone her colleague Joseph. She looked up his number but, before she dialled the number, she got distracted by her husband and had a short conversation with him. When she looked at her phone, she had completely forgotten Joseph's number. Use your knowledge of the multi-store model to explain why Laura forgot Joseph's number. (4 marks)

 **Exam Hint** Sometimes students get confused with application questions such as this and focus on SR, attention and STM, when in fact the answer requires students to focus on STM, rehearsal and LTM.

9 Many cognitive psychologists have criticised the multi-store model, as it fails to explain memory in everyday life. For example, students often spend hours and hours reading through their revision notes but struggle to retain the information. However, these same students can remember information found on social media even though they have only seen it once. Explain why this information presents a criticism of the multi-store model of memory. (4 marks)

 **Exam Hint** To answer this question effectively, students are required to focus on the two types of information (revision notes and social media) and link these to a criticism of the MSM.

10 Outline and evaluate the multi-store model of memory. Refer to research evidence in your answer. (4 marks)

 **Exam Hint** With this question, students need to be careful when evaluating the model. For example, when using case studies (HM, KF or Clive Wearing), students need to ensure that they explain whether these support the MSM.

CHAPTER 2 TYPES OF LONG-TERM MEMORY

Specification: Types of long-term memory: episodic, semantic and procedural.

What you need to know

Outline and evaluate the different types of long-term memory, including:
- Episodic
- Semantic
- Procedural

Introduction to Types of Long-Term Memory

Atkinson & Shiffrin's (1968) multi-store model is often criticised for being too simplistic. Although they made a distinction between a sensory register (SR), short-term memory (STM) and **long-term memory (LTM)**, they provided no detail of the memory processing within each store. The Working Memory Model (WMM) proposed by Baddeley and Hitch (1974) divided STM into two separate subcomponents: the phonological loop and the visuo-spatial sketchpad [see next section]. In addition, psychologists have suggested that there are multiple types of LTM, including: **episodic**, **sematic** and **procedural**.

Although there are at least three types of LTM (episodic, semantic and procedural), all long-term memories are categorised as either **explicit** (**declarative**) or **implicit** (**non-declarative**). Explicit memories include knowledge of events and facts (knowing that), whereas implicit memories are skilled behaviours (*knowing how*), which are largely unconscious.

Episodic Memory

Episodic memory is a type of explicit memory, which includes memories of personal experiences (episodes), such as your first day at school or when you last visited the doctor. These memories are more complex than you might consider and have three specific elements including details of the event; the context; and emotions, which are all interwoven to provide a single memory.

The strength of episodic memories is determined by the strength of the emotions experienced when the memory is coded, and a conscious effort is required to retrieve them. Episodic memories are associated with the hippocampus, although other areas of the brain regions are associated with coding (prefrontal cortex).

Semantic memory

Semantic memory is also a type of explicit memory, which includes memory for knowledge, facts, concepts and meaning about the world around us. For example, knowing that London is the capital of England is an example of a semantic memory and so too is knowing that the legal age to drive in the UK is 17 years old.

Semantic memories often *start* as episodic memories, as we acquire knowledge based on our personal experiences, but they are not 'time-stamped' in the same way, nor do they remain closely associated with a particular event (episode). Like episodic memories, the strength of semantic memories is determined by the strength of the emotions experienced when the memory is coded, although semantic knowledge is often less personal and can relate to abstract concepts such as language and maths. However, semantic memories are generally stronger in comparison to episodic and are associated with the temporal lobe.

Procedural memory

Procedural memory is a type of implicit memory, which includes the memory of how to perform certain tasks, actions or skills, such as swimming, reading and writing which have become 'automatic'.

Procedural memories are implicit and therefore difficult to explain in words to someone else. They are often acquired through repetition and practice, for example, when we learn to ride a bike or drive a car. Many procedural memories are formed early in life, for example, walking. These must become like second nature to us so that we can focus our direct attention on other everyday tasks we perform at the same time. (Imagine walking with a friend and having to stop every time you wanted to say something!) Procedural memories are associated with the cerebellum and motor cortex.

	Episodic	Semantic	Procedural
Explicit/Implicit	Explicit	Explicit	Implicit
Type	Personal experiences	Knowledge	Performed tasks or skills
Brain Region	Hippocampus	Temporal lobe	Cerebellum and motor cortex

Evaluating Types of Long-Term Memory

- One strength of this area is that there is objective evidence to support different types of long-term memories. For example, brain scans have shown that different parts of the brain are active when accessing episodic, semantic and procedural memory. Episodic memory has been associated with the hippocampus and temporal lobe; semantic memory is also associated with the temporal lobe; and procedural memory is associated with the cerebellum and motor cortex. Brain scan research suggests that different brain regions are responsible for the different types of LTM, supporting the idea that our LTM is made up of at least three distinct categories.

- One strength is that there is research to support the distinction between implicit and explicit LTM. For example, the case study of patient HM (Milner, 1962). Patient HM suffered from severe epilepsy and underwent surgery, which involved the removal of his hippocampus, to alleviate the symptoms. His STM remained intact; however, he was unable to transfer certain types of information to his LTM. Milner discovered that HM was able to learn procedural (implicit) tasks, but not episodic or semantic (explicit) information. HM was able to learn a mirror-tracing task, where you copy an image while looking in a mirror and retain the skill without forgetting. However, he had no knowledge of ever previously completing the mirror-tracing task. Therefore, HM was able to demonstrate his procedural memory through implicit behaviour, despite being unable to recall his experience explicitly.

- Further support for the distinction of implicit and explicit memory comes from a separate case study of Patient PM (Finke *et al.* 2012), a cellist who suffered from amnesia because of a virus. Like patient HM, his implicit memory (episodic and semantic) memory was affected, but his procedural memory for reading and performing music remained intact. PM demonstrates a clear distinction between different types of LTM. Although both HM and PM provide support for the distinction of separate types of LTM, evidence from case studies must be treated with caution. It is difficult to establish exactly which brain regions are affected in patients with brain damage and damage to a particular region (for example, the hippocampus) does not necessarily mean that region is associated with a particular type of memory.

- The strength of understanding different types of memory means it allows for the development of helpful real-world applications. Belleville *et al.* (2006) compared the performance of older people suffering from mild cognitive impairment who received memory training with that of a control group who did not. It was found that participants in the experimental group performed better on a test of episodic memory. This suggests that being able to identify different types of LTM can provide psychologists with the opportunity to improve people's lives though devising appropriate treatments.

Extension Evaluation: Issues and Debates

- One strength of research into this area is that it adopts both a nomothetic and an idiographic approach since it attempts to generate universal laws of cognitive processes including our different types of long-term memories (episodic, semantic and procedural), but also uses case studies, such as in the case of Patient HM and Clive Wearing.

- One limitation of research into this area is that it can be reliant on case studies. The case studies are examples of socially sensitive research, which is why HM's identity was hidden from all but the researchers until he died in 2008. It could be argued that the same protection should have been extended to Clive Wearing.

POSSIBLE EXAM QUESTIONS

1 Identify which of the following is not a type of long-term memory. (1 mark)
- **a Episodic**
- **b Sensory**
- **c Semantic**
- **d Procedural**

2 Identify and explain one difference between episodic and procedural memory. (3 marks)

 **Exam Hint** Remember if asked in the exam to compare different types of memory, use conjunctives such as 'however', 'alternatively', 'in contrast' or 'on the other hand' to illustrate a clear comparison between your two definitions.

3 Define what is meant by the terms semantic and episodic memory. Outline one difference between these types of long-term memory. (3 marks)

 **Exam Hint** You must spot the two parts to this question. Firstly, you have to define the terms, and secondly, you have to offer a difference.

4 Distinguish between procedural and semantic memory. (3 marks)

 **Exam Hint** Students need to ensure that they do not confuse semantic memory with semantic processing. Students often struggle to achieve three marks on questions like this. An easy way to pick up the third mark is to distinguish between these types of memory by referring to declarative and non-declarative memory.

5 Many studies of brain-damaged patients follow a case study methodology. Outline one strength and one limitation of the case study method. (3 marks)

 **Exam Hint** Your strength and limitation do not need to be related to each other, but it can sometimes provide clarity to your evaluation if they do. You could consider population validity, socially sensitive research, or other points.

6 Sarah suffered brain damage following a car accident a few years ago. Sarah was, and still is, a very talented artist specialising in intricate watercolour paintings. Though she can still create the same masterpiece repeatedly within minutes, she does not recall ever learning this artistic skill. Using your knowledge and understanding of different types of long-term memory, explain how the car accident has affected Sarah's memory. (3 marks)

 **Exam Hint** You are required to demonstrate AO2 application skills here. Your answer to this question must be in the context of the question, and you must do more than merely refer to Sarah.

7 Briefly outline what is meant by episodic, semantic and procedural memory. (6 marks)

 **Exam Hint** Each outline needs to include some elaboration to reach full marks. You can use examples to support your answer, but do not become distracted by them, and do not become reliant on them for an answer.

8 Outline and evaluate different types of long-term memory. (16 marks)

 **Exam Hint** Spend approx. 20-25 minutes on this question and ensure that you address both of the assessment objectives in your answer. You must provide a coherent and detailed outline of the types of LTM, and then a coherent, elaborate, well-structured evaluation.

CHAPTER 3 THE WORKING MEMORY MODEL

Specification: The working memory model: central executive, phonological loop, visuo-spatial sketchpad and episodic buffer. Features of the model: coding and capacity.

Introduction to the Working Memory Model

The **Working Memory Model (WMM)** was proposed by Baddeley & Hitch (1974) as a way of explaining some of the research findings that could not be accounted for by the multi-store model (MSM), for example, dual-task studies.

The WMM focuses on short-term memory (STM) and Baddeley and Hitch put forward a multi-component system, which consists of a **central executive, phonological loop** and **visuospatial sketchpad**.

The central executive is the 'boss' of the WMM. It controls attention and directs information to the two slave systems, the phonological loop and visuospatial sketchpad. The central executive can process information from any sensory modality.

The phonological loop is a temporary storage system for verbal information (held in a speech-based form) which has two components, the articulatory control process (the 'inner voice') and the phonological store (the 'inner ear'). The articulatory control process allows for subvocal repetition of acoustic information, and the phonological store is a temporary storage space for coding acoustic information, which has a limited capacity.

The visuospatial sketchpad is a temporary storage system for visual and spatial information which also has two components, the inner scribe and the visual cache. The inner scribe deals with the manipulation of mental images and the visual cache has a limited capacity for coding visual and spatial information.

The episodic buffer binds and integrates information from all the components and passes the information to long-term memory (LTM). It therefore codes both visual and acoustic information, but also has a limited capacity.

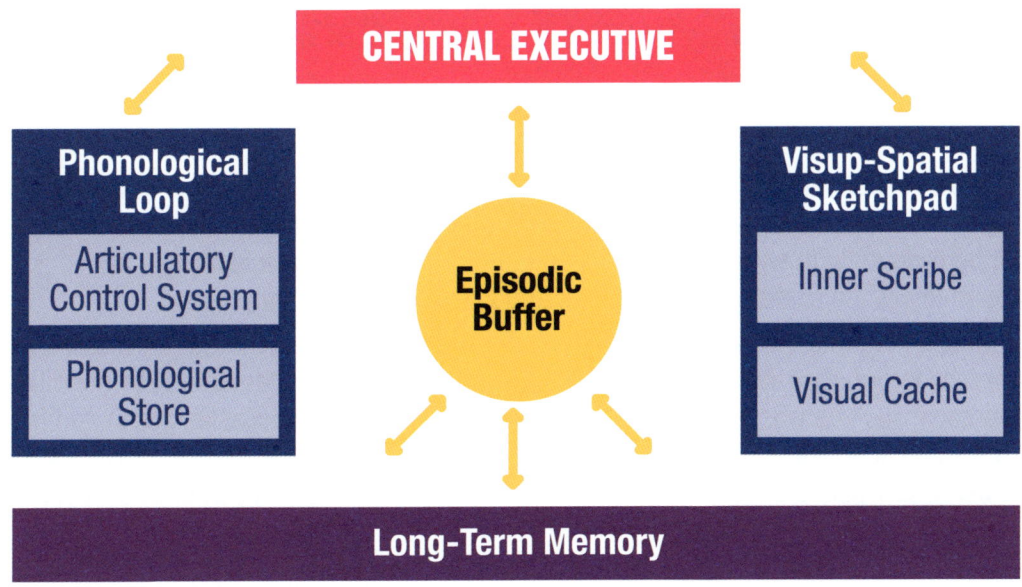

	Central Executive	Phonological Loop	Visuospatial
Function	Control centre of the WMM; supervisory function and controls the slave systems	Temporary storage system for verbal information, held in speech-based form	Temporary storage system for visual and spatial information
Capacity	Limited capacity	Limited capacity	Limited capacity
Coding	Any sensory modality	Acoustic information	Visual and spatial information

Evaluating the Working Memory Model

- One strength of the WMM is that there are case studies to support it. For example, Patient KF was injured in a motorcycle accident. Following his accident, KF was able to recall stored information from his LTM; however, he had issues with his STM. He was able to remember visual images, including faces, but was unable to remember sounds (acoustic information). This suggests that there are at least two components within STM, one component for visual information and one for acoustic information. The research into KF supports the WMM and the idea of two slave systems, the phonological loop and the visuo-spatial sketchpad, therefore providing support to the WMM and the idea of a multi-component STM system.

- Further support for the WMM comes from dual-task studies by Baddeley and Hitch (1976). Dual-task studies require participants to complete two tasks at the same time. In one condition, participants may be required to complete two acoustic-based tasks, such as simultaneously remembering a series of digits and completing a verbal reasoning task. In another condition, participants may be required to complete one acoustic-based task and one visual-based task, for example, remembering a series of digits and copying a drawing. When both tasks require the participants to use their phonological loop, their ability to perform the tasks is impaired. However, when one task requires the participant to simultaneously use their phonological loop (remembering a series of numbers) and the other requires their visuospatial sketchpad (copying a drawing) then their performance is not impaired. Dual-task studies provide evidence for the existence of multiple components within our STM and support the idea of a separate phonological loop and visuo-spatial sketchpad.

- One limitation of the WMM is that the link between the WMM and LTM is not fully explained. The WMM provides a detailed description of our STM, but limited information on how information is processed and transferred from STM to LTM and back again. Therefore, the WMM is an incomplete model of memory and other theories/models are required to gain a complete picture of this complex cognitive phenomenon. However, it can be argued that the WMM only ever intended to explain the functions of STM, rather than LTM.

- One limitation of the WMM is that there is very little known about the central executive. Although research into the WMM exists more broadly, there is a lack of research about the central executive and its role. Considering that this is arguably the most important system in the WMM, this casts doubt on what we truly understand about the WMM and STM.

Extension Evaluation: Issues and Debates

- One limitation of the research into WMM is that it often demonstrates experimental reductionism. It attempts to examine complex behaviours by relying on isolated variables operationalised in laboratory experiments. By breaking down behaviours in this way, and attempting to quantify memory, it is likely that conclusions will not be holistic enough to explain something as complex and individual as memory.

- Furthermore, the WMM adopts a nomothetic approach since it attempts to generate universal laws regarding how STM processes information, based on dual-task studies conducted under laboratory conditions. Using an idiographic approach, such as was used by Oliver Sacks with Clive Wearing (Sacks, 2007) and Brenda Milner with HM (Milner, 1957), can shed light on how STM loss can vary between people, with HM's STM severely affected, but still not as badly as Wearing's, despite the almost total removal of his hippocampus and surrounding tissue.

POSSIBLE EXAM QUESTIONS

1 Select one study of the working memory model and outline what the participants were required to do. (2 marks)

 **Exam Hint** Students should mention what participants are required to do in both conditions of an experiment (e.g. dual-task studies by Baddeley and Hitch) to achieve both marks available.

2 Dual-task studies often find that when participants are required to carry out two visual tasks at the same time, they perform less well than participants who carry out one visual task and one verbal task. Use your knowledge of the working memory model to explain this finding. (3 marks)

 **Exam Hint** Students can often write too much for a three-mark question. Students should aim to write 50–75 words for a question such as this. Furthermore, students are required to explain why participants who complete two visual tasks perform less well, rather than provide a detailed description of dual-task studies.

3 Briefly outline the working memory model. (4 marks)

 **Exam Hint** Students are often inclined to describe the WMM in far too much detail. Students should aim to write approximately 75–100 words maximum on a four-mark question. Furthermore, answers that only name the components and do not describe the processes of the model will fail to access the higher mark band.

4 Abdul is an experienced taxi driver and can drive safely and with little difficulty whilst holding engaging conversations with his passengers. Shafia is a new driver and has only had five lessons; she finds driving difficult. While concentrating on the pedals and steering, Shafia often misses the instructions her driving instructor provides. With reference to the working memory model, explain the difference displayed between Abdul and Shafia. (4 marks)

 **Exam Hint** You should spot that this question requires you to demonstrate your A02 application skills, and your answer should be in the context of the people in the stem.

5 Joseph can listen to music while writing his homework. However, he finds it difficult to do it while talking to his dad, Jim on the phone. Use your knowledge of the working memory model to explain why Joseph can perform the first two tasks easily but struggles to perform the second two tasks. (4 marks)

 **Exam Hint** You should read a stem more than once so that you are equipped to 'problem solve' what areas of your knowledge you can apply to the stem.

6 Outline one strength and one limitation of the working memory model. (4 marks)

 **Exam Hint** Students are not credited for stating that the WMM does not explain LTM or that it is based on case studies (it is not – a lot of the research is laboratory-based). However, students can gain credit for stating that the link between the working memory model and LTM is not fully explained.

7 The working memory model consists of the central executive, the phonological loop and the visuospatial sketchpad. Briefly outline each of these components. (6 marks)

- **Central Executive**
- **Phonological Loop**
- **Visuo-Spatial Sketchpad**

 **Exam Hint** Some students simply name the subcomponents of the phonological loop and visuospatial sketchpad and this is not enough to achieve top marks. Furthermore, students often struggle with outlining the function of the central executive, even for two marks. Read over this area before attempting the question.

8 Outline and evaluate the working model of memory. (16 marks)

 **Exam Hint** Students are required to outline the processes involved in the WMM rather than limiting their descriptions to the components of the model. For example, it is not enough to say that the phonological loop consists of two subsystems. Furthermore, for the evaluation element of this question, students tend to outline research support (e.g. dual-task studies) but fail to explain how/why these provide support for the WMM.

CHAPTER 4 EXPLANATIONS FOR FORGETTING

Specification: Explanations for forgetting: proactive and retroactive interference and retrieval failure due to the absence of cues.

What you need to know

Outline and evaluate different explanations for forgetting, including:
- Proactive interference
- Retroactive interference
- Retrieval failure

Outline and evaluate research examining different explanations for forgetting

Introduction to Forgetting

Long-term memories are not always remembered, and forgetting can occur for different reasons. Psychologists have suggested different explanations for forgetting: **proactive interference, retroactive interference** and **retrieval failure** due to the absence of cues.

Interference

Interference theories suggest that forgetting is caused by *competing memories*, either because existing memories interfere with the learning of new information (proactive interference) or because new information interferes with previously learnt information (retroactive interference).

Proactive Interference

Proactive interference occurs when old information stored in long-term memory (LTM), interferes with the learning of new information. This usually occurs when the new information is similar to the old information. An everyday example of proactive interference is when you get a new mobile phone number: your memory for your old number will disrupt your attempts to remember your new number.

Research: Keppel & Underwood (1962)

Aim: To investigate the effect of proactive interference on LTM.

Method: In an experiment that is very similar to that conducted by Peterson & Peterson (1959), participants were presented with meaningless three-letter consonant trigrams (for example, THG) at different intervals (3, 6, 9 seconds, etc.) To prevent rehearsal the participants had to count backwards in threes before recalling.

Results: Participants typically remembered the trigrams that were presented first, irrespective of the interval length.

Conclusion: The results suggest proactive interference occurred, as memory for the earlier consonants (which had transferred to LTM) interfered with the memory for new consonants, due to the similarity of the information presented.

Retroactive Interference

Retroactive interference occurs when the learning of new information interferes with the recall of old information from LTM. For example, once you have learned your new mobile number, it is often very difficult to recall your old number.

Research: Baddeley & Hitch (1977)

Aim: To investigate retroactive interference in everyday memory.

Method: The sample comprised rugby union players who had played every match in the season and players who had missed some games due to injury. The length of time from the start to the end of the season was the same for all players, and players were asked to recall the names of the teams they had played against earlier in the season.

Results: The players who had played the most games forgot more games than those who had played fewer games due to injury.

Conclusion: Baddeley and Hitch concluded that this was the result of retroactive inference, as the learning of new information (new team names) interfered with the memory of old information (earlier team names).

Evaluating Interference Theories

- One strength of the research by Baddeley and Hitch is that the findings are supported by other researchers, for example, **McGeoch and McDonald (1931)**. In their experiment, participants were given a list of ten adjectives to learn (list A). Once these adjectives were learnt, participants were then given one of six other lists (list B) to learn, which varied in terms of its similarity to the original. McGeoch and McDonald found recall was worse when lists A and B were closest in similarity. This supports the idea of retroactive interference because the more similar the new material is to the previously learnt material, the greater the interference.

- One limitation is that interference does not explain all types of forgetting. Although interference research (proactive and retroactive) provides insight into one type of forgetting, it only explains memory for similar information. For example, the results of Baddeley and Hitch demonstrate retroactive interference in rugby union players trying to recall team names from earlier in the season and Keppel and Underwood demonstrate proactive interference when trying to learn three-letter consonant trigrams. Both of these examples highlight the interference effects of very similar information and therefore this research is limited in its real-world application and is unable to explain forgetting in other situations.

- One limitation of interference theory is that it is often supported by problematic research. For example, many studies lack ecological validity. Most of the research examining interference is carried out in a laboratory, for example, Keppel and Underwood (1962) and McGeoch and McDonald (1931), while using particularly meaningless stimuli, such as three-letter consonant trigrams or simple word lists. As a result, these findings do not represent everyday examples of interference and are limited in their application to everyday human memory.

Retrieval Failure due to Absence of Cues

Another type of forgetting occurs when information cannot be retrieved because of insufficient cues to trigger memory. Tulving and Thomson (1973) proposed the encoding specificity principle and argued that memory is most effective when information that was present at the time of coding is also present at the time of retrieval. Furthermore, they suggested that environmental cues and mental cues aid recall. Environmental cues include the room in which you learn information, and mental cues include your emotional state. Consequently, there are two types of retrieval failure due to the absence of cues: 1) context-dependent failure and 2) state-dependent failure.

Context-Dependent Forgetting

Context-dependent failure occurs when environmental cues are missing, and state-dependent failure occurs when an individual's emotional state is different when trying to recall information.

Research: Godden & Baddeley (1975)

Aim: To investigate the effect of contextual cues on recall (i.e. would memory for words learned and recalled in the same environment be better than memory for words learned and recalled in different environments?)

Method: Their sample comprised 18 participants (13 males and 5 females) from a university diving club, who were divided into four conditions: 1) learning words on land and recalling on land; 2) learning words on land and recalling underwater; 3) learning underwater and recalling underwater; and 4) learning underwater and recalling on land. The experiment was a repeated measures design with each participant taking part in all four conditions, over four separate days. In all four conditions, participants were presented with 38 words, which they heard twice. After hearing all 38 words the participants were instructed to write all the words they could remember, in any order.

Results: The words learned underwater were better recalled underwater and words learned on land were better recalled on land. Forgetting occured most when the context during the time of learning was different at the time of recall. For example, learning on land and recalling in water.

Conclusion: It is, therefore, reasonable to conclude that a change or absence of environmental cues (context) can contribute to forgetting.

Mean number of words recalled

Learning Environment	Land		Underwater		Total
	Mean Recall Score	SD	Mean Recall Score	SD	
Land	13.5	5.8	8.6	3.0	22.1
Underwater	8.4	3.3	11.4	5.0	19.8
Total	21.9	-	20.0	-	-

Evaluating Context-Depending Forgetting

- One limitation of Godden and Baddeley's research is that they did not control many other variables. The divers took part in the experiment at different times of the day and different diving locations. Therefore, each diver would have experienced other contextual cues, which may have affected their memory. Therefore, we are unable to conclude whether the results of Godden & Baddeley's research are due to the on-land/underwater contextual cues, or another contextual cue provided by the different time of day or diving location.

- Another limitation of the supporting research is that Godden & Baddeley used a repeated measures design, as each diver took part in all four conditions. It is possible that the divers worked out the aim of the experiment and displayed demand characteristics or order effects. By the fourth trial, the participants may have demonstrated practice effects where their recall improved because of completing the experiment multiple times or even fatigue effects where their results declined as a result of boredom. Furthermore, with a sample of just 18 divers, the conclusions drawn should be treated with caution. Additionally, the context examined in their study is extreme and provides little insight into context-dependent forgetting in everyday life.

State-Dependent Forgetting

When the emotional state that an individual is in serves as an aid to memory recall, there is a risk that state-dependent forgetting will occur when the same psychological state is not experienced. This is often the case with alcohol intoxication and the absence of accurate memories when sober.

Research: Carter & Cassaday (1998)

Aim: Carter & Cassaday (1998) examined state-dependent forgetting using antihistamine drugs. These are typically administered as hay fever relief to sufferers but are also known for their sedating effect. This can make the individual feel drowsy, and therefore not as alert as they would normally be, providing a comparison to everyday non-drug-induced behaviour.

Procedure: Participants were tasked with learning a list of words and excerpts from a text and then asked to recall the information at a later point. There were four conditions in their experiment:

1 learn the words/text after taking antihistamines and recall them after taking antihistamines

2 learn the words/text without antihistamines and recall them without antihistamines

3 learn the words/text after taking antihistamines and recall without antihistamines

4 learn the words/text without antihistamines and recall them after taking the antihistamines

Findings: In the conditions where the learning and recalling states matched (i.e. after taking the drugs on both occasions and not taking the drugs on both occasions) memory was improved. Consequently, when the physiological state of the participants was different recall was significantly poorer.

Conclusion: When the physiological/emotional cues that are present at the time of encoding are missing at the time of retrieval (recall), state-dependent forgetting is likely to occur.

Evaluating State-Depending Forgetting

- There is research support for the effect of state-dependent retrieval failure, which occurs when an individual's emotional state at the time of learning is different to their emotional state at the time of recall. For example, Goodwin *et al.* (1969), asked male volunteers to remember lists of words when they were either drunk or sober. The participants were then asked to recall the words 24 hours later, in either a drunk or sober state. The results of Goodwin *et al.* support Godden and Baddeley, as words learned when drunk were better recalled when drunk, and words learnt when sober were better recalled when sober. These results support the idea of state-dependent retrieval failure and demonstrate the power of 'state' in recalling information.

- There is research support for state-dependent forgetting using a range of different substances to create an alternative state of consciousness. Darley *et al.*, (1973) researched the impact of marijuana on an individual's recollection. It was found that individuals who were under the influence of marijuana when they put money in a 'safe place' were less able to recall where this location was once, they were no longer under the influence of the drug. This evidence adds weight to the argument that the emotional and physiological state that a person is in at the time of encoding is important at the time of retrieval.

- One limitation of this theory of forgetting is that there are issues with determining a cause-and-effect relationship with retrieval failure as an explanation of forgetting. Nairne (2002) criticised research in this area suggesting that there is merely a correlation between cues present at the time of encoding and cues present at the time of later retrieval. He goes further and suggests that the cues do not in themselves cause the retrieval failure (or success) but are simply associated with it. This would mean that the cue-dependent (context and state) explanations of forgetting due to retrieval failure are, in fact, circular rather than linear and psychologists are unable to conclude whether a lack of cues causes retrieval failure.

Extension Evaluation: Issues and Debates

- One limitation of these theories of forgetting is that they use a nomothetic approach to establish general laws regarding forgetting, but often by generalising from small studies with homogeneous samples. An idiographic approach investigating forgetting using participants of different ages and cultures may give more insight into this complex phenomenon.

- One limitation of Baddeley & Hitch's (1977) research is that it showed gender bias. They investigated retroactive interference using an all-male sample of rugby players and then applied their findings outside of this target population to include females. This is an example of beta-bias, which occurs when researchers minimise possible differences between females and males and assume that research carried out on one gender may be universally applied to the other.

POSSIBLE EXAM QUESTIONS

1 Explain what is meant by the term interference. (2 marks)

 **Exam Hint** Students need to be careful with their use of terminology for this question. Phrases like 'old memories get mixed up with new' are not explicit enough and students should be encouraged to write clear and concise definitions.

2 Select one study in which interference was investigated. Briefly explain what the participants had to do. (2 marks)

 **Exam Hint** Many students fail to achieve the full two marks because they do not provide clear details about the two separate conditions of the experiment. When explaining what participants had to do, students need to make it clear what distinguishes the two conditions investigating interference.

3 Select one study in which retrieval failure was investigated. Briefly explain what the participants had to do. (2 marks)

 **Exam Hint** Your answer should focus on 'what the participants had to do' which refers to part of the methodology. Refrain from giving an overview of the whole study, since it will not be creditable.

4 Briefly outline one strength of interference theory as an explanation for forgetting. (3 marks)

 **Exam Hint** You must elaborate on your strength to reach full marks. You will know several strengths, so think carefully and be selective. Choose a point that you can elaborate on clearly and with appropriate specialist terminology.

5 Briefly outline one limitation of interference theory as an explanation for forgetting. (3 marks)

 **Exam Hint** A common response to limitations of interference theory is to focus on ecological validity. However, students often struggle to develop this point beyond a single statement like 'studies lack ecological validity'. Students need to explicitly state how/why such studies do not apply to everyday examples of human memory for full credit to be awarded.

6 Explain what is meant by the terms proactive and retroactive interference. (4 marks)

 **Exam Hint** For each term, you need to offer a little elaboration. Do not rely on examples, and take great care to not mix the two up!

7 Outline one study that demonstrates interference. (6 marks)

 **Exam Hint** For 6 marks, your answer needs to include sufficient detail of a recognisable and relevant study. You can include information about the sample, aims, procedures, and results.

8 Outline one study that demonstrates how the absence of cues may lead to retrieval failure. (6 marks)

 **Exam Hint** Make sure you choose a study that matches this explanation of forgetting. The question does not mention whether you are to focus on state or context cues, so the decision is yours.

9 Marcus is studying for his upcoming A-Level language examinations. He revises Spanish followed by Italian one evening and then gets mixed up. For example, he recalled the Spanish word for 'dog' instead of the Italian word for 'dog'. Marcus's father helps him with learning his key vocabulary and when Marcus is unable to remember a word, his father gives him the first letter which helps him to recall the word correctly. Discuss two explanations for forgetting and refer to Marcus in your answer. (16 marks)

 **Exam Hint** You should spend 20-25 minutes on this question. The command word 'discuss' means you are required to demonstrate both knowledge and evaluation/critical thinking. You are also required to demonstrate your A02 application skills and do more than merely refer to Marcus.

10 Outline and evaluate how retrieval failure due to the absence of cues leads to forgetting. (16 marks)

 **Exam Hint** When talking about retrieval failure, make sure you focus on forgetting, rather than why we use cues to remember. Offer 3-4 evaluation paragraphs and use specialist terminology throughout your answer.

CHAPTER 5 EYEWITNESS TESTIMONY

Specification: Factors affecting the accuracy of eyewitness testimony: misleading information, including leading questions and post-event discussion; anxiety.

What you need to know

Explain what is meant by the term eyewitness testimony

Outline and evaluate research examining the accuracy of eyewitness testimony, including:
- Misleading information
  - Post event discussion
  - Leading questions
- Anxiety

Introduction to Eyewitness Testimony

An **eyewitness testimony** is the evidence given in court or a police investigation by someone who has witnessed a crime or accident. For many years psychologists have investigated the factors that can affect the accuracy of eyewitness reports, to ensure that the evidence provided during investigations is reliable and accurate. Psychologists have identified several factors that can have a detrimental effect on the accuracy of eyewitness reports, including:

- **Misleading Information: leading questions:** questions that lead witnesses to alter their memory for events. For example, a question that asks 'did you see the knife?' may lead witnesses to remember a knife, even if there was no knife.

- **Misleading Information: post-event discussions:** when people talk about what they have witnessed (e.g. co-witnesses) they contaminate their memory for the event, and can recall information that they did not see, or alter information they did see.

- **Anxiety:** a heightened emotion that can affect the accuracy of eyewitness testimonies. For example, the presence of a weapon can lead to high anxiety and poorer recall.

MISLEADING INFORMATION – LEADING QUESTIONS

Research: Loftus & Palmer (1974) – Experiment 1

Aim: To investigate the effect of leading questions on the accuracy of eyewitness testimony.

Method: The sample was 45 American students, who were divided into five groups of nine. In an independent measures design, all the participants watched a video of a car crash and were then asked a specific question about the speed of the cars. Loftus & Palmer manipulated the verb used in the question, for example: "How fast were the cards going when they *smashed/ collided/ bumped/ hit/ contacted* with each other?"

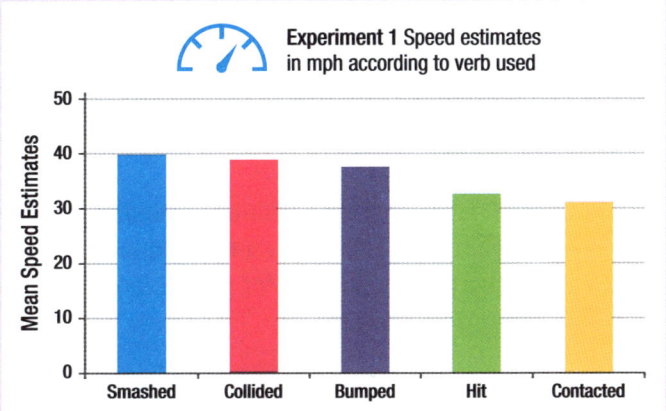

They found that the estimated speed was affected by the verb used. For example, participants who were given the verb 'smashed' reported an average speed of 40.5 mph, whereas participants who were given the word 'contacted' reported an average speed of 31.8 mph, an overall difference of 8.7 mph.

Conclusion: The results show clearly that the accuracy of eyewitness testimony is affected by leading questions and that a single word in a question can significantly affect the accuracy of our judgements.

Research Loftus & Palmer (1974) – Experiment 2

Aim: To investigate further how leading questions can affect eyewitness testimony.

Method: Loftus & Palmer used a different sample of 150 American students, who were divided into three evenly-sized groups. All of the students watched a one-minute video depicting a car accident and were then given a questionnaire to complete. One group was asked: "How fast were the cars going when they smashed into each other?" Another group was asked: "How fast were the cars going when they hit each other?" The final group (control) was not asked about the speed of the vehicles. One week later the participants returned and were asked a series of questions about the accident. The critical question was: "Did you see any broken glass?" There was no broken glass in the video clip.

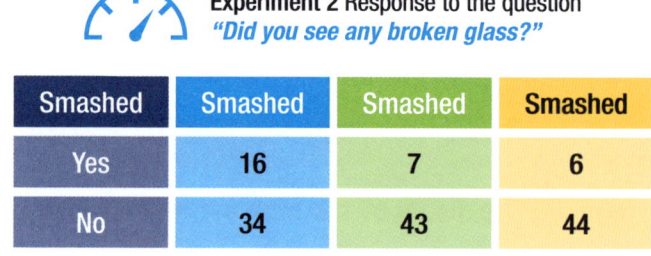

Experiment 2 Response to the question *"Did you see any broken glass?"*

Smashed	Smashed	Smashed	Smashed
Yes	16	7	6
No	34	43	44

Results: 32% of the participants who were previously questioned using the verb smashed reported seeing broken glass; 14% of the participants who were previously questioned using the verb hit reported seeing broken glass; and 12% of the control group reported seeing broken glass.

Conclusion: The participants who were questioned previously using the verb smashed were significantly more likely to report seeing the broken glass, because of the earlier leading question. The verb smashed has connotations of faster speeds and broken glass and this question led the participants to report seeing something that was not present. Their memory of the original event was distorted by the question used one week earlier, demonstrating the power of leading questions.

Evaluating Loftus & Palmer

- One limitation is that the research has questionable ecological validity. On the one hand, questioning participants about everyday events like a car crash appears to be a genuine measure of eyewitness testimony. However, the participants watched a video of a car crash and witnessed the events unfold from start to finish. In everyday reports of car accidents, witnesses rarely see the whole event; they are either involved in the event directly or see a small part of the event happen in their peripheral vision. Therefore, their results do not reflect everyday car accidents and we are unable to conclude if eyewitnesses to real accidents, who would have a stronger emotional connection to the event, would be susceptible to leading questions in the same way.

- A second weakness of Loftus & Palmer's research is that their study lacks population validity. Their two experiments consisted of 45 and 150 students from the University of Washington. It is reasonable to argue that the students in their experiment were less experienced drivers, who may be less accurate at estimating speeds. Consequently, we are unable to generalise the results to other populations, for example, older and more experienced drivers, who may be more accurate in their judgement of speeds and therefore not as susceptible to leading questions.

- One strength is that Loftus & Palmer's research took place in a university laboratory and was therefore highly controlled. This high degree of control reduces the chance of extraneous variables, increasing the validity of the results. Furthermore, it is easy for psychologists to replicate their research, to see if the same results are achieved with a different population.

MISLEADING INFORMATION – POST-EVENT DISCUSSION

One source of misleading information comes from leading questions, as detailed above. However, misleading information in the real world can come from other sources, for example, other witnesses (co-witnesses), when they discuss the details of a crime or accident, following an incident. This is known as post-event discussion.

Research: Gabbert *et al.* (2003)

Aim: To investigate the effect of post-event discussion on the accuracy of eyewitness testimony.

Method: The sample comprised 60 students from the University of Aberdeen and 60 older adults recruited from a local community.

Participants watched a video of a girl stealing money from a wallet. The participants were either tested individually (control group) or in pairs (co-witness group). The participants in the co-witness group were told that they had watched the same video; however, they had seen different perspectives of the same crime and only one person had witnessed the girl stealing. Participants in the co-witness group discussed the crime together. All the participants then completed a questionnaire, testing their memory of the event.

Results: 71% of the witnesses in the co-witness group recalled information they had not seen and 60% said that the girl was guilty, even though they had not seen her commit a crime.

Conclusion: These results highlight the issue of post-event discussion and the powerful effect this can have on the accuracy of eyewitness testimony.

Evaluating Gabbert *et al.* (2003)

- One limitation of the study is that it has questionable ecological validity. The participants in the co-witness condition witnessed different perspectives of the same crime, as would typically be the case in real-life crimes. However, as in Loftus and Palmer's research, these witnesses knew they were taking part in an experiment and were more likely to have paid close attention to the details of the video clip. Therefore, these results do not reflect everyday examples of crime, where witnesses may be exposed to less information.

- One strength of the study is that it has good population validity. Gabbert *et al.* tested two different populations, university students and older adults, and found little difference between these two conditions. Therefore, her results provide good population validity and allow us to conclude that post-event discussion affects younger and older adults similarly.

- One limitation of the study is that although Gabbert *et al.*'s results provide insight into the effect of post-event discussion on the accuracy of eyewitness testimony, we are unable to explain why the distortion to memory occurs. The distortion could be the result of poor memory, where people assimilate new information into their accounts of the event and are unable to distinguish between what they have seen and what they have heard. On the other hand, it could be that the distortion occurs due to conformity and social pressure from the co-witness. Further research is required to answer this question.

ANXIETY

Loftus (1979) reported the findings of **Johnson & Scott (1976)** who experimented to see if anxiety affects the accuracy of eyewitness testimony and facial recognition.

Research Loftus (1979) / Johnson & Scott (1976)

Aim: To investigate whether anxiety affects the accuracy of eyewitness testimony.

Method: Participants were invited to a laboratory where they were told to wait in the reception area. A receptionist who was seated nearby excused herself to run an errand, leaving the participant alone. The experiment used an independent group design, as participants were then exposed to one of two conditions:

1. In the 'no-weapon' condition, participants overheard a conversation in the laboratory about equipment failure. Thereafter, an individual (the target) left the laboratory and walked past the participant holding a pen, with his hands covered in grease.

2. In the 'weapon' condition, participants overheard a heated exchange and the sound of breaking glass and crashing chairs. This was followed by an individual (the target) running into the reception area, holding a bloodied letter-opening knife.

Both groups were then shown 50 photographs and asked to identify the person who had left the laboratory. The participants were informed that the suspect may, or may not, be present in the photographs.

Results: Those who had witnessed the man holding a pen correctly identified the target 49% of the time, compared to those who had witnessed the man holding a knife, who correctly identified the target 33% of the time.

Conclusion: Loftus claimed that the participants who were exposed to the knife had higher levels of anxiety and were more likely to focus their attention on the weapon and not the face of the target, a phenomenon known as the weapon focus effect. Therefore, the anxiety associated with seeing a knife reduces the accuracy of eyewitness testimony.

Evaluation of Anxiety as a Factor Affecting EWT

- One limitation is that there is contradictory evidence. A real-life case study by Yuille & Cutshall (1986) contradicts the results of Loftus (1979) and the weapon focus effect. Yuille & Cutshall investigated the effect of anxiety in a real-life shooting, in which one person was killed and another person seriously wounded. 21 witnesses were originally interviewed by investigating police and 13 witnesses, aged between 15 and 32, agreed to take part in Yuille and Cutshall's follow-up research interview, 4–5 months later. Yuille and Cutshall found that the 13 witnesses who took part in the follow-up interview were accurate in their eyewitness accounts five months later, and little change was found in their testimonies. All the major details of their reports remained the same and only minor details, including estimates of age, height and weight, changed. Furthermore, the witnesses avoided responding in a biased way to leading questions and the anxiety experienced at the time of the event had little or no effect on their subsequent memory of the event. These results refute the weapon focus effect and the results of Loftus (1979) and show that in real-life cases of extreme anxiety, the accuracy of eyewitness testimony is not affected.

- Another limitation is that the research has been criticised for lacking ecological validity. Although the participants were waiting in the reception area outside the laboratory, they may have anticipated that something was going to happen, which could have affected the accuracy of their judgements. Furthermore, the results from real-life case studies (see above) refute the findings of Loftus and suggest that her results do not represent real-life cases of extreme anxiety.

- A final criticism of the research is that numerous ethical guidelines were broken. The participants were deceived about the nature of the experiment and not protected from harm. The research exposed some of the participants to a man holding a bloodied knife, which could have caused extreme feelings of anxiety. This is an issue, as these participants may have left the experiment feeling exceptionally stressed and anxious, especially if they, or someone they knew, had been involved in a knife crime.

Extension Evaluation: Issues and Debates

- Loftus & Palmer's (1974) research is, like much research into memory, an example of experimental reductionism: the complex process of memory after a film of what would in real-life be a traumatic event is reduced to the effect of the wording of a leading question (IV) on the eyewitness memory (DV). The research also suffers from cultural bias, as samples of participants were from either Britain or the America. However, it has helped to develop the Cognitive Interview Technique, which aims to improve the accuracy of eyewitness testimonies and replace outdated, unhelpful, standard interview techniques.

- Loftus & Palmer, Yuille & Cutshall and Johnson & Scott all use a nomothetic approach to try to establish universal laws regarding eyewitness testimony, but their claims are based on small, non-representative samples.

POSSIBLE EXAM QUESTIONS

1 Outline what is meant by the term leading questions. Provide an example to support your answer. (3 marks)

 **Exam Hint** You do not need to use research in your response, although you could use some as your example.

2 Explain how leading questions might affect the accuracy of eyewitness testimony. (3 marks)

 **Exam Hint** Rather than explain what a leading question is, or rely on examples, you must explain HOW they affect eyewitness testimonies. We know they can be detrimental, but you must explain how this occurs.

3 Explain how post-event discussion could lead to an inaccurate eyewitness report. (3 marks)

 **Exam Hint** As with Q2, you must focus on HOW eyewitness reports are impacted by post-even discussion, rather than merely state what a post-event discussion is.

4 Explain how anxiety might affect the accuracy of eyewitness testimony. (3 marks)

 **Exam Hint** You can explain the positive or negative effects of anxiety in your responses here, as long as you are addressing the demands of the question.

5 Some psychologists argue that it is better to conduct research into eyewitness testimony in the real world, rather than a laboratory. Explain this view. (3 marks)

 **Exam Hint** While many students can refer to the notion of ecological validity, they fail to elaborate their answers enough to achieve all three marks. Sound answers to this question will draw on research to support their knowledge.

6 Outline what research has found in relation to the effect of misleading information on eyewitness testimony. (4 marks)

 **Exam Hint** Students need to ensure that they focus their answers on the question. Many students provide a full outline of research (e.g. Loftus & Palmer) and don't shape their answer to the results and conclusion/s of the research. This question explicitly states: 'What research has found' and therefore answers should not include the aim and procedure.

7 Outline one study that has investigated the effect of anxiety on eyewitness testimony. (4 marks)

 **Exam Hint** Students who fail to score full marks on these questions often omit the IV/DV in their answers. As a rule, when students outline a study within a short-answer question they should provide clear and concise details in relation to the key aspects of the methodology.

8 Outline how one study has investigated the accuracy of eyewitness testimony. (4 marks)

 **Exam Hint** Students often fail to pick up on the word 'how' in questions such as this and therefore provide a detailed summary of research which does not answer the question. Students need to ensure that they provide details of the methodology specifically.

9 A young man is being questioned by police about an incident he witnessed in his local area. An argument took place outside the pub, followed by a violent attack. The police later discovered a knife at the scene.

Policeman: "Did you see the knife the perpetrator was holding?".

Young man: "I don't remember; there was probably a knife, yes. I was so shocked and scared it's hard to remember exactly what happened. It's all my friends have been talking about for the past couple of days so I'm not sure exactly what I remember seeing".

Discuss factors that affect the reliability of eyewitness testimony. Refer to the scenario in your answer. (16 marks)

 **Exam Hint** Discuss means you should demonstrate your knowledge and evaluation skills, however you must also apply your knowledge to the context of the incident in the stem. Read the stem several times and annotate what could be relevant to the question.

10 Outline and evaluate research into the effect of anxiety on eyewitness testimony. (16 marks)

Exam Hint When you write your evaluation for this question, you could consider research that supports claims that anxiety is detrimental, and counter it with research that claims anxiety can have positive effects (or no effect!).

CHAPTER 6 IMPROVING THE ACCURACY OF EYEWITNESS TESTIMONY

Specification: Improving the accuracy of eyewitness testimony, including the use of the cognitive interview.

Introduction to the Cognitive Interview

The **cognitive interview** was developed in 1985, in response to criticisms of the traditional police interview. **Fisher *et al.* (1987)** studied police interviews in Florida and found that witnesses were often presented with a series of short, closed questions, which attempted to elicit facts. Furthermore, the police would often ask questions in a sequence that was not synchronised with the events that had taken place.

As a result, **Geiselman *et al.* (1985)** developed the cognitive interview, identifying four key principles that they believed would enhance recall, including:

- **Context reinstatement (CR)**
- **Report everything (RE)**
- **Recall from changed perspective (CP)**
- **Recall in reverse order (RO)**

CR is when a person mentally recalls the context of the event. For example, a person might recall the time of day, the weather, who they were with, or even their feelings. These details can then act as a trigger, to help the person recall more information. There are clear links here between this and context-dependent and state-dependent remembering.

RE is when a person recalls every detail they can remember, even those that may seem trivial.

CP is when a person considers the event from someone else's point of view. For example, they might consider what the offender saw.

Finally, **RO** is where a person recalls the events in reverse chronological order.

Research: Geiselman (1985)

Aim: To examine the effectiveness of the cognitive interview.

Method: A sample of 89 students watched a video of a simulated crime. Two days later the students were interviewed using the standard police interview or the cognitive interview.

Results: The students who were interviewed using the cognitive interview recalled significantly more correct information than those interviewed using the standard interview. In addition, the number of errors (incorrect items recalled) by both groups was similar.

Conclusion: The cognitive interview is effective in improving the quantity of information recalled.

	Cognitive Interview	Standard Interview
Average number of correct items recalled	41.5	29.3
Average number of incorrect items recalled	7.3	6.1

Evaluating the Cognitive Interview

- One strength of the cognitive interview is that the results of Geiselman have been supported by other research, including Fisher *et al.* (1989). These researchers examined the effectiveness of the cognitive interview in real police interviews. 16 experienced detectives recorded a selection of their interviews, using a standard interviewing technique. The detectives were then divided into two groups. One group was trained to use the cognitive interview, while the other (control) group continued using the standard interview. After training, their subsequent interviews were recorded and analysed. The trained detectives elicited 46% more information after their cognitive interview training, in comparison to the control group. Where it was possible to confirm the information, over 90% of it was found to be accurate. These results support the findings of Geiselman, using real police interviews, and provide support for the effectiveness of the cognitive interview.

- One limitation is that although the cognitive interview increases the quantity of information recalled, research has found that the cognitive interview is still susceptible to misleading information. Centofanti & Reece (2006) showed participants a video of a bank robbery and then provided participants with a misleading or neutral post-event summary. On average the participants who were questioned using a cognitive interview recalled 35% more information. However, the participants in both conditions were equally susceptible to misleading information. Therefore, although the cognitive interview enhances the quantity of information recalled, interviewers need to be careful that participants are not exposed to misleading information in the form of leading questions or post-event discussions.

- Although research supports the effectiveness of the cognitive interview, Kebbell & Wagstaff (1996) have found that police typically use interviewing techniques that limit the quantity of information provided, rather than those that improve accuracy. Furthermore, the cognitive interview requires special training, and many police forces have not provided more than rudimentary training, which explains why the cognitive interview is not readily used.

Extension evaluation: issues and debates

- In common with much of the research into memory, research into police interview procedures, and the subsequent development and testing of the cognitive interview technique, suffers from experimental reductionism: there could be many explanations for difficulties that victims and eyewitnesses experience in recalling an event, apart from the technique that is used to interview them. For example, the research does not address a possible culture bias, in that the researchers and the participants are from a Western culture, but the results are taken to apply to all cultures.

POSSIBLE EXAM QUESTIONS

1 Identify and explain two techniques used in the cognitive interview. (4 marks)

 **Exam Hint** You can choose any two techniques to include in your answer. Whatever ones you choose, make sure you elaborate on them and explain what they involve and/or how they help.

2 Outline how the cognitive interview differs from a standard interview. (4 marks)

 **Exam Hint** This is an evaluative question, so is asking you to compare the two types of interviews. Avoid merely outlining each one. Instead, clarify differences and explain them in some detail.

3 Outline how the cognitive interview can be used to improve the accuracy of eyewitness testimony. (4 marks)

 **Exam Hint** The word 'how' means you should focus on how the interview can be used in the real world. For example, what might a witness experience in a cognitive interview? How might a police officer use the cognitive interview technique?

4 Molly was waiting for her bus home one night when she witnessed a violent attack involving a stabbing. A man came out of the pub across the road, followed by another man who pulled a knife out of his pocket and stabbed the first man in the back before running across the road towards Molly. When he noticed that she had seen him, he turned left and ran off down an alleyway. The police officer who questioned Molly about the incident used cognitive interview techniques. Explain how the officer could use the cognitive interview to improve the accuracy of Molly's account. (6 marks)

 **Exam Hint** This question requires students to go beyond the scenario outlined in the stem and use their knowledge of the cognitive interview to explain how the police could use these techniques. Responses which explain how the police could use the different techniques, such as context reinstatement by forming an example question that the police could use, will be more likely to gain access to the higher mark boundaries.

5 Discuss the use of the cognitive interview as a means of improving the accuracy of eyewitness testimony. (16 marks)

 **Exam Hint** Spend approx. 20-25 minutes on this question, and ensure your evaluation is elaborate, effective, and includes specialist terminology. Use research that says the cognitive interview is effective, and counter it with contradictory evidence.

EXAM STYLE QUESTIONS ON MEMORY

Describe and evaluate the multi-store model of memory.
Refer to evidence in your answer. (16 marks)

Atkinson & Shiffrin (1968) proposed the multi-store model (MSM) which suggests that memory is made up of three components: sensory register (SR), short-term memory (STM) and long-term memory (LTM). The model proposes that memories are formed sequentially, and information passes from one component to the next, in a linear fashion.

Information enters the sensory register via our senses such as sound or sight. The sensory register has a very limited duration of less than one second. Information that is attended to is passed to STM, which has a limited capacity of 7+/-2 'chunks' of information and a limited duration of approximately 20 seconds. Information in our STM is coded in an acoustic format. Thereafter, rehearsed information is transferred to LTM, which has an unlimited capacity and a lifetime duration. Information in LTM is coded semantically and can be retrieved from LTM to STM when required.

Support for the MSM comes from the case of Clive Wearing, who contracted a virus that caused severe amnesia (memory loss). Following the virus, Wearing could only remember information for 20–30 seconds; however, he was able to recall information from his past, for example, his wife's name. Furthermore, Wearing was unable to transfer information from his STM to his LTM, but he was able to retrieve some information successfully. Wearing's case supports the idea that memories are formed by passing information from one store to the next, in a linear fashion, and that damage to any part of the MSM can cause memory impairment.

While the case of Clive Wearing supports the MSM, other case studies refute the model. For example, the case of patient KF, who was injured in a motorcycle accident. Following his accident, KF could recall stored information from his LTM; however, he had issues with his STM. KF was also able to remember visual images, including faces, but was unable to remember sounds (acoustic information). This suggests that there are at least two components within STM, one component for visual information and one for acoustic information, which suggests that the MSM may provide an overly simplified account of STM.

Further support for the MSM comes from psychological studies. For example, Miller (1959) supports the idea of a limited capacity of 7+/-2 chunks of information in STM; Peterson & Peterson (1959) support the idea of a limited duration in STM of approximately 20 seconds and Bahrick (1975) supports the idea of a lifetime duration in LTM. These studies all support the different elements of the MSM and therefore suggest that the model is an accurate representation of human memory. However, research examining the MSM is a clear example of experimental reductionism, as it attempts to explain a complex behaviour by relying on isolated variables, operationalised in laboratory experiments such as the capacity of STM, or duration of STM. However, as memory is a complex phenomenon, many psychologists argue that reducing memory to isolated variables undermines the complexity of human memory and does not provide us with a comprehensive understanding of memory in everyday contexts.

Finally, evidence from brain scans has shown that different areas of the brain are active when performing STM tasks (hippocampus and subiculum) and LTM tasks (motor cortex). This suggests that different brain regions are responsible for the different components of the MSM, supporting the idea that our memory is made up of discrete stores.

Specialist terminology associated with the model is identified from the offset.

Accurate and detailed overview of the components of the multi-store model, including both the components and processes (e.g. attention, rehearsal, etc.)

Relevant research support for this model of memory utilising an appropriate case study to illustrate the point.

A second case study is used to provide balance to the argument.

An excellent use of research support, combined with sound knowledge of issues and debates, serves to enhance the evaluative commentary.

An interesting piece of evidence is presented in the final evaluation point about localisation of memory in different brain regions.

Examiner style comments: *Mark band 4*

This is a sufficiently detailed and accurate account of the multi-store model of memory, providing the appropriate content for a 16-mark essay question. The evaluation is well detailed, thorough and effective including one embedded reference to a relevant issue and debate to ensure the answer sits firmly within the top mark band.

Describe and evaluate types of long-term memory. (16 marks)

Psychologists have suggested that there are at least three types of long-term memory, including: episodic, semantic and procedural. Episodic memory is a type of explicit memory, which includes memories of personal experiences, such as the first day at school. Episodic memories have three elements: details of the event; context; and emotions, which are interwoven. The strength of episodic memories is determined by the strength of the emotions experienced when the memory is coded, and a conscious effort is required to retrieve them.

Semantic memory is also an explicit memory, which includes memory for knowledge, facts, concepts and meaning about the world around us, for example, knowing that London is the capital of England. These memories are not 'time-stamped' or linked to an event.

Procedural memory is a type of implicit memory, which includes memory of how to perform certain tasks, actions or skills such as swimming, reading and writing, which become 'automatic'. They are implicit and therefore difficult to explain in words to someone else. They are acquired through repetition and practice and many procedural memories are formed early in life, for example, walking.

Brain scans provide support for different types of LTM. Research suggests that different parts of the brain are active when accessing episodic, semantic and procedural memories. Episodic memories have been associated with the hippocampus and temporal lobe; semantic memories are also associated with the temporal lobe; and procedural memories are associated with the cerebellum and motor cortex. Brain scan research suggests that different brain regions are responsible for the different types of LTM, supporting the idea that LTM is made up of at least three distinct categories.

Support for the distinction between implicit and explicit LTM comes from the case study of patient HM (Milner, 1962). HM suffered from severe epilepsy and underwent surgery, which involved the removal of his hippocampus, to alleviate the symptoms. His STM remained intact; however, he was unable to transfer certain types of information to his LTM. Milner discovered that HM could learn procedural (implicit) tasks, but not episodic or semantic (explicit) information. HM could complete a mirror tracing task, where an image is copied whilst looking in a mirror and retain the skill without forgetting. However, he had no knowledge of ever completing the mirror tracing task. Therefore, HM could demonstrate his procedural memory through implicit behaviour, despite being unable to recall his experiences explicitly. HM therefore provides further evidence for the distinction between different types of LTM, namely implicit and explicit.

Understanding different types of memory allows for the development of helpful real-world applications. Belleville *et al.* (2006) compared the performance of older people suffering from mild cognitive impairment who received memory training with that of a control group who did not. It was found that participants in the experimental group performed better on a test of episodic memory. This suggests that being able to identify different types of LTM can provide psychologists with the opportunity to improve people's lives though devising appropriate treatments to help alleviate the problems associated with age-related memory impairment.

Episodic memory is described in detail using specialist vocabulary.

A second type of long-term memory is outlined in a concise manner.

A third, and final, type of long-term memory is presented and well explained.

The evaluative commentary is enhanced and elaborated efficiently. Specialist terminology is used throughout.

Appropriate evidence is presented to support the distinction between implicit and explicit long-term memories utilising HM's case study well.

The evaluative commentary is concluded with an interesting real-world application, drawing upon psychological evidence to support the point.

Examiner style comments: *Mark band 4*

This is a well-detailed essay which explains the three types of long-term memories named on the specification. A good balance of breadth and depth across the three concepts is achieved. The evaluation is effective and the use of specialist terminology is consistent throughout to ensure that this is a secure mark band 4 response.

Discuss what psychological research has shown about working memory. In your answer, refer to theory and/or evidence. (16 marks)

The working memory model (WMM) was proposed by Baddeley and Hitch (1974) to account for some of the limitations of the multi-store model. They felt that short-term memory consists of multiple stores and not just one unitary store and that STM is an active process (hence the name 'working' memory).

The central executive controls the WMM and directs attention to one of three slave systems. The phonological loops deal with auditory information and contain the phonological store which holds the words you hear and the articulatory control process which allows for maintenance rehearsal of acoustic information. The visuospatial sketchpad (VSS) is used for the planning of spatial tasks. The VSS contains the visual cache which stores visual information and the inner scribe which deals with spatial relationships and stores the arrangement of objects in the visual field. In 2000, Baddeley added the episodic buffer which is a general store for both visual and acoustic information. The purpose of the episodic buffer is to integrate information from the other three components and transfer information to long-term memory.

One strength of the working memory models comes from dual-task studies. Baddeley and Hitch (1976) found that when two tasks require the participants to use their phonological loop, their ability to perform the tasks is impaired. However, when one task requires the participant to simultaneously use their phonological loop (remembering a series of numbers) and the other requires their visuospatial sketchpad (copying a drawing) then their performance is not impaired. This provides support to the model and the existence of multiple components within our STM system.

Further support for the WMM comes from case studies. For example, the case of patient KF, who was injured in a motorcycle accident, demonstrates that STM consists of multiple components. Following his accident, KF could recall stored information from his LTM; however, he had issues with his STM. He was also able to remember visual images, including faces, but was unable to remember sounds (acoustic information). This suggests that there are at least two components within STM, one component for visual information (visuospatial sketchpad) and one for acoustic information (phonological loop), thus supporting the WMM.

However, one limitation of the working memory model is that it focuses on short-term memory and does not explain much about long-term memory. The working memory model provides a detailed description of our short-term memory, but no information on the sensory register and long-term memory. The WMM is not a complete model of memory and is therefore limited in its application to everyday human memory and is unable to explain how information arrives at our working memory and how information is stored in the long term. However, the WMM did not intend to explain long-term memory, so this criticism can be challenged.

Research examining the WMM often demonstrates experimental reductionism, as it attempts to examine complex behaviour by relying on isolated variables operationalised in laboratory experiments. Furthermore, the WMM adopts a nomothetic approach since it attempts to generate universal laws regarding how STM processes information, based on dual-task studies conducted under laboratory conditions. Using an idiographic approach, such as was used by with Clive Wearing can shed light on how STM loss can vary between people.

An interesting start to the essay outlining the rationale and purpose of the model.

Specialist terminology is used with accuracy.

Additional information about the WMM completes the detailed outline.

Evaluative commentary is kicked off with relevant research support from dual task studies.

Evaluation is developed with further support from an appropriate case study.

Evaluation is balanced with a limitation of the working memory model.

A strong end to the essay with creditworthy reference to issues and debates related directly to the question.

Examiner style comments: *Mark band 4*

This is a well-detailed and accurate account of the working memory model and its contribution to cognitive psychology. The evaluation is well-detailed, thorough and effective, drawing on a range of points to create balance between strengths and limitations. The use of specialist terminology is excellent and consistent from start to finish.

Marcus is studying for his language exams. He revises Spanish followed by Italian one evening and then gets mixed up. For example, he recalled the Spanish word for 'dog' instead of the Italian word for 'dog'. Marcus finds that when he is at home revising with his father, his knowledge and memory are significantly better than when he is in the classroom completing a test in silence.

Discuss two explanations for forgetting and refer to Marcus in your answer. (16 marks)

One explanation for forgetting is proactive interference. It occurs when old information stored in long-term memory (LTM) interferes with the learning of new information. This usually occurs when the new information is similar to the old information.

One explanation for forgetting is identified and explained.

Keppel And Underwood (1962) investigated the effect of proactive interference on LTM whereby participants were presented with meaningless three-letter consonant trigrams at different intervals. To prevent rehearsal the participants had to count backwards in threes before recalling. Participants typically remembered the trigrams that were presented first, irrespective of the interval length. The results suggest proactive interference occurred, as memory for the earlier consonants (which had transferred to LTM) interfered with the memory for new consonants, due to the similarity of the information presented.

Relevant research is described with accuracy. Link to proactive interference explanation is explicit.

In Marcus's case, the Spanish word for dog that he learned first will have been replaced with the newer Italian word for dog which he revised later. The two words are probably similar which explains why he is struggling to recall the Italian word.

Appropriate material from the scenario is applied to the psychological theory.

Interference research is often criticised for being artificial and lacking ecological validity. Most of the research examining interference is carried out in a laboratory, for example, Keppel and Underwood (1962) and McGeoch and McDonald (1931), while using particularly meaningless stimuli, such as three-letter consonant trigrams or simple word lists. As a result, these findings do not represent everyday examples of interference and are limited in their application to everyday human memory. Despite this criticism, the results do appear to support Marcus's case, as he is forgetting two very similar pieces of information, in the same way, that Keppel and Underwood's participants were attempting to recall similar three-letter consonant trigrams.

Methodological critique of the research commences the evaluative commentary in an effective manner.

Reference to the scenario is consistent throughout the response.

Another type of forgetting occurs when information cannot be retrieved because of insufficient cues to trigger memory. Tulving and Thomson (1973) proposed the encoding specificity principle and argued that memory is most effective when information that was present at the time of coding is also present at the time of retrieval. Furthermore, they suggested that environmental cues and mental cues aid recall. Environmental cues include the room in which you learn information, and mental cues include your emotional state.

A second type of forgetting is presented and well explained, using specialist terminology with confidence.

Godden and Baddeley (1975) provided research support for the idea of retrieval failure. They studied the effect of contextual cues on recall to investigate whether memory for words learned and recalled in the same environment is better than memory for words learned and recalled in different environments. Their sample consisted of divers who learned words on land or underwater and then recalled the words in the same or opposite context. They found that words learned underwater were better recalled underwater and words learned on land were better recalled on land. This supports the idea that environmental cues aid recall.

Appropriate research is drawn upon to support the description.

It is no surprise that Marcus finds it easier to recall information when at home because his revision and learning take place at home and therefore the context of being at home aids his recall. It also explains why he struggles with recalling information when completing a test in silence, because the context, the classroom, and the condition, being in silence, are different to the context and condition in which the learning took place.

The essay concludes with another successful attempt at applying knowledge and understanding of forgetting to the case of Marcus.

Examiner style comments: *Mark band 4*

This is a well-structured essay which clearly addressed all of the AO1, AO2 and AO3 elements that this question demands. An accurate and well-detailed account of two types of forgetting are presented, using key terms effectively to demonstrate sound knowledge and understanding. A range of effective evaluation points are used to support or critique the explanations. The application to the scenario with Marcus is clear, coherent and focused on the material provided, culminating in a great response.

Describe and evaluate how retrieval failure due to the absence of cues leads to forgetting. (16 marks)

Tulving and Thomson (1973) proposed the encoding specificity principle which argued that memory is most effective when information that was present at the time of coding is also present at the time of retrieval. They suggested that environmental and mental cues aid recall. Consequently, there are two types of retrieval failure due to the absence of cues: context-dependent failure and state-dependent failure. Context-dependent failure occurs when environmental cues are missing, and state-dependent failure occurs when an individual's emotional state is different.

Godden and Baddeley (1975) investigated the effect of contextual cues on recall using a sample of 18 participants from a university diving club. They were divided into four conditions: 1) learning words on land and recalling on land; 2) learning words on land and recalling underwater; 3) learning underwater and recalling underwater; and 4) learning underwater and recalling on land. It was found that words learned underwater were better recalled underwater and words learned on land were better recalled on land. These results provide clear support for the idea of context-dependent retrieval failure and the idea that context can aid recall.

While Godden and Baddeley provide support for the idea of context-dependent retrieval failure, their research has numerous methodological flaws. They used a repeated measures design, and each diver took part in all four conditions. It is possible that the divers worked out the aim of the experiment and displayed demand characteristics or order effects. By the fourth trial the participants may have demonstrated practice effects where their recall improved because of completing the experiment multiple times, or even fatigue effects where their results declined because of boredom. Furthermore, with a sample of just 18 divers, the conclusions drawn should be treated with caution. Additionally, the context examined in their study is extreme and provides little insight into context-dependent forgetting in everyday life.

Other researchers have sought to examine the effect of state-dependent retrieval failure, which occurs when an individual's emotional state at the time of learning is different to their emotional state at the time of recall.

For example, Goodwin *et al.* (1969) asked male volunteers to remember lists of words when they were either drunk or sober. The participants were then asked to recall the words 24 hours later, in either a drunk or a sober state. The results of Goodwin *et al.* support Godden and Baddeley, as words learned when drunk were better recalled when drunk and words learnt when sober were better recalled when sober. These results support the idea of state-dependent retrieval failure and demonstrate the power of 'state' in recalling information.

Theories of forgetting, including context and state-dependent retrieval failure take a nomothetic approach to establish general laws regarding forgetting that apply to all humans. However, such research is often based on small sample sizes and does not provide an accurate reflection of memory in all humans in all situations. Consequently, an idiographic approach investigating forgetting using participants of different ages and cultures may give more insight into this complex phenomenon.

An interesting start to the essay drawing on appropriate theories from the outset.

Specialist terms are explained well.

Accurate account of Godden and Baddeley's study to complete the description element of this response.

The evaluative commentary is effectively developed using critiques of the methodology.

The evaluative commentary is further enhanced by additional research support which is appropriate to the demands of the question.

Confident understanding of issues and debates is demonstrated here and applied well to the theories of forgetting.

Examiner style comments: *Mark band 4*

This is a detailed and accurate essay examining forgetting due to retrieval failure. Although both context and state-dependent forgetting are referred to initially, the focus is on context-dependent forgetting for the main part. This is appropriate given the number of marks available for AO1. The use of specialist terminology, including a reference to ethical issues, is impressive. The evaluation is focused, thorough and effective to provide a sound response overall.

A man is being questioned by police about an incident he witnessed outside a pub in his local area. An argument took place outside the pub, followed by a violent attack. The police later discovered a knife at the scene. "Did you see the knife the perpetrator was holding", asked the police. "I don't remember; however, there probably was a knife", replied the man. "I was so shocked and scared it's hard to remember exactly what happened. It's all my friends have been talking about over the past couple of days, so I'm not sure what I saw".

Discuss factors that affect the reliability of eyewitness testimony. Refer to the scenario in your answer. (16 marks)

Two key factors that affect the reliability of eyewitness testimony (EWT) are leading questions and anxiety. Loftus & Palmer (1974) examined three groups of students who watched a one-minute video of a car accident. One group was asked: "How fast were the cars going when they smashed into each other?", while the other group was asked the same question with the verb 'hit'. One week later they were asked: "Did you see any broken glass?", despite the fact there was none. 32% of participants in smashed condition said yes, compared to 14% (hit) and 12% (control), suggesting that misleading questions can significantly affect the reliability of EWT and make people report seeing things that they didn't.

Accurate and detailed outline of relevant research on misleading questions directly related to the question.

One limitation of Loftus and Palmer's research is that their study lacks population validity. Their sample consisted of 150 American students. It is reasonable to argue that the students in their experiment were less experienced drivers, who may be less accurate at estimating speeds. Consequently, we are unable to generalise the results to other populations, for example, older and more experienced drivers, who may be more accurate in their judgement of speeds and therefore not as susceptible to leading questions.

Evaluation of the research is effective and uses specialist terminology well.

Just like Loftus & Palmer's experiment, the man questioned in the extract was asked a leading question: "Did you see the knife the perpetrator was holding?" The use of the word 'the' is leading the man to think there was a knife even though he wasn't originally sure. This is evident by his confused/uncertain reply where he says there 'probably' was one.

Excellent engagement with the scenario extracting appropriate material to support the point being made.

Johnson & Scott (1976) investigated the effect of anxiety on the reliability of EWT. Participants were invited to a laboratory where they were exposed to one of two conditions in which a person, known as the target, left the laboratory either holding a pen or a bloodied knife. The participants were then shown 50 photos and asked to identify the person. Those in the pen condition correctly identified the target 49% of the time, compared to just 33% in the knife condition. Loftus claimed that the participants who were exposed to the knife had higher levels of anxiety and were more likely to focus their attention on the weapon, known as the weapon focus effect, suggesting that anxiety can affect the reliability of EWT.

Research on weapon focus demonstrates a sound understanding of this area in psychology.

However, a real-life case study by Yuille and Cutshall (1986) contradicts the results of Loftus (1979). Yuille and Cutshall investigated the effect of anxiety in a real-life shooting and found that the 13 witnesses who took part in the follow-up interview were accurate in their eyewitness accounts five months later, and little change was found in their testimonies. All the major details of their reports remained the same suggesting that the anxiety experienced at the time of the event had little or no effect on their subsequent memory of the event and the reliability of their EWT.

An interesting evaluation point comparing results of a real-life case study.

The man outlined in the extract was anxious ("I was so shocked") and this could have affected the reliability of his EWT. However, it is unclear whether or not he saw a knife and therefore the weapon focus effect would not apply to this situation. The results of Yuille and Cutshall, which are based on real-world crimes, suggest that the anxiety experienced would not affect the reliability of his EWT and that his memory of the event would remain accurate both immediately after and up to five months later.

Effective reference to the scenario again showing that all elements of the question have been addressed fully.

Examiner style comments: *Mark band 4*

This is a well-structured essay which provides an accurate and detailed account of two factors – misleading questions and anxiety – which can affect eyewitness testimony. The essay is clear and coherent, and specialist terminology is used throughout the outline and evaluation sections with confidence. Application to the scenario is well considered and draws on appropriate material from the scenario to illustrate the point being made.

Outline and evaluate research into the effects of leading questions on eyewitness testimony. (16 marks)

Loftus & Palmer (1974) investigated the effect of leading questions on the accuracy of eyewitness testimony using a sample of American students. All participants watched a video of a car crash and were then asked a specific question about the speed of the cars. Loftus and Palmer manipulated the verb used in the question, for example: "How fast were they cars going when they *smashed/ collided/ bumped/ hit/ contacted* with each other?"

They found that the estimated speed was affected by the verb used. For example, participants who were given the verb 'smashed' reported an average speed of 40.5 mph, whereas participants who were given the word 'contacted' reported an average speed of 31.8 mph, an overall difference of 8.7 mph. These results show clearly that the accuracy of eyewitness testimony is affected by leading questions and that a single word in a question can significantly affect the accuracy of our judgements.

Loftus and Palmer's research has questionable ecological validity. On the one hand, questioning participants about everyday events like a car crash appears to be a genuine measure of eyewitness testimony. However, the participants watched a video of a car crash and witnessed the events unfold from start to finish. In everyday reports of car accidents, witnesses rarely see the whole event; they either are involved in the event directly or see a small part of the event happen in their peripheral vision. Therefore, their results do not reflect everyday car accidents and we are unable to conclude if eyewitnesses to real accidents, who would have a stronger emotional connection to the event, would be susceptible to leading questions in the same way.

A second weakness of Loftus and Palmer's research is that their study lacks population validity. Their two experiments only used American university students as participants. It is reasonable to argue that the students in their experiment were less experienced drivers, who may be less accurate at estimating speeds. Consequently, we are unable to generalise the results to other populations, for example, older and more experienced drivers, who may be more accurate in their judgement of speeds and therefore not as susceptible to leading questions.

However, Loftus and Palmer's research took place in a university laboratory and was therefore highly controlled. This high degree of control reduces the chance of extraneous variables, increasing the validity of the results. Furthermore, it is easy for psychologists to replicate their research, to see if the same results are achieved with a different population. While the highly controlled laboratory conditions are considered a strength, Loftus & Palmer's (1974) research is an example of experimental reductionism: the complex process of memory after watching a film, for what would in real life be a traumatic event, is reduced to the effect of the wording of a leading question (IV) on the eyewitness memory (DV). Real-life EWT accounts are affected by a multitude of factors and while these results highlight the potential impact of misleading questions, the results may not reflect everyday EWT accounts which could be affected by other factors including anxiety, post-event discussion and age.

A key piece of research investigating this area of psychology is identified and well explained.

Accurate and detailed knowledge and understanding of the procedure and findings is demonstrated.

Effective evaluative commentary is created using methodological arguments.

The discussion is enhanced with a further valid limitation of Lotus and Palmer's research.

The evaluation is balanced with a strength of the laboratory method.

The commentary is concluded with an interesting reference to reductionism and how this applies to leading questions and eyewitness testimony in everyday life.

Examiner style comments: *Mark band 4*

This is a highly detailed and accurate essay examining the effect of leading questions on the accuracy of eyewitness testimony. One relevant study conducted by Loftus and Palmer is presented in great depth, appropriate for the approximate 150-word outline recommended. The use of specialist terminology is impressive. The evaluation is focused, thorough and effective, incorporating issues and debates effortlessly.

Discuss research into the effects of misleading information on the accuracy of eyewitness testimony. (16 marks)

Misleading information incorporates misleading questions and post-event discussion. Loftus & Palmer (1974) examined the effect of misleading questions by using three groups of students who watched a one-minute video of a car accident. One group was asked: How fast were the cars going when they smashed into each other?", while the other group was asked the same question but with the verb 'hit'. One week later they were asked: "Did you see any broken glass?", despite the fact there was none. 32% of participants in smashed condition said yes, compared to 14% (hit) and 12% (control). These results suggest that misleading questions can significantly affect the reliability of EWT and make people report seeing things they didn't witness.

One limitation of Loftus and Palmer's research is that their study lacks population validity. Their experiment consisted of 150 American students. It is reasonable to argue that the students in their experiment were less experienced drivers, who may be less accurate at estimating speeds. Consequently, we are unable to generalise the results to other populations, for example, older and more experienced drivers, who may not be affected by misleading questions in the same way.

Furthermore, Loftus and Palmer's research has questionable ecological validity. On the one hand, questioning participants about everyday events like a car crash appears to be a genuine measure of eyewitness testimony. However, the participants watched a video of a car crash and witnessed the events unfold from start to finish. In everyday reports of car accidents, witnesses rarely see the whole event; they are either involved in the event directly or see a small part of the event happen in their peripheral vision. Therefore, their results may not reflect everyday car accidents, and we are unable to conclude if the effect of leading questions is the same outside the laboratory.

Gabbert *et al.* (2003) investigated the effect of post-event discussion. Her participants watched a video of a girl stealing money. However, participants in the co-witness group were told that they had watched the same video when they had, in fact, seen different perspectives. 71% of the witnesses in the co-witness group recalled information they had not seen and 60% said that the girl was guilty, despite not having seen her commit a crime. These results highlight the issue of post-event discussion and the powerful effect this can have on the accuracy of eyewitness testimony.

Although Gabbert's results provide insight into the effect of post-event discussion on the accuracy of eyewitness testimony, we are unable to conclude why this distortion occurs. The distortion could be the result of poor memory, where people assimilate new information into their accounts of the event and are unable to distinguish between what they have seen and what they have heard. On the other hand, it could be that the distortion occurs due to conformity and social pressure from the co-witness. Therefore, further research is required in the real world to demonstrate the exact effect of misleading information on the accuracy of EWT.

Explanation of the specialist terminology sets scene for the rest of the essay.

Accurate and detailed account of this key research study on misleading questions.

A well-elaborated validity argument is presented as the first evaluation point.

A second form of validity is brought into question regarding Loftus and Palmer's research.

Thorough outline of key research study into the effects of post-event discussion.

The essay concludes with an interesting point which considers the origins of memory distortion.

Examiner style comments: *Mark band 4*

This essay demonstrates sound knowledge understanding of the effects of misleading information on eyewitness testimony. The discussion shows appreciation for the role of misleading questions and post-event discussion, striking a good balance between the two concepts. The evaluation is effective, interesting and focused on the demands of the question.

Outline and evaluate research into the effects of anxiety on the accuracy of eyewitness testimony. (16 marks)

Loftus (1979) reported Johnson and Scott's (1976) experiment investigating anxiety and the accuracy of eyewitness testimony. The participants were invited to a laboratory where they were told to wait in the reception area. The participants were then exposed to one of two conditions: 1) Participants overheard a conversation about equipment failure followed by an individual leaving the laboratory holding a pen. 2) Participants overheard a heated exchange and the sound of breaking glass and crashing chairs followed by an individual running into the reception area, holding a bloodied letter-opening knife.

Clarity is established about the origin of the key research.

Both groups were shown 50 photographs and asked to identify the person who had left the laboratory. Those who had witnessed the man holding a pen correctly identified the individual 49% of the time. Those who had witnessed the man holding a knife correctly identified the target 33% of the time. Loftus suggested the participants who saw the knife experienced more anxiety and therefore focused their attention on the weapon, not the face, which is called the weapon focus effect.

Accurate and detailed outline of the procedure.

Sound knowledge and understanding of the main findings is evident.

However, a real-life case study by Yuille and Cutshall (1986) contradicts the weapon focus effect. They investigated the effect of anxiety in a real-life shooting, in which one person was killed and another person seriously wounded. 21 witnesses were originally interviewed by investigating police and 13 witnesses, aged between 15 and 32, agreed to take part in Yuille and Cutshall's follow-up research interview, 4–5 months later. They found that the 13 witnesses who took part in the follow-up interview were accurate in their eyewitness accounts five months later, and little change was found in their testimonies. All the major details of their reports remained the same and only minor details, including estimates of age, height and weight, changed. Furthermore, the witnesses avoided responding in a biased way to leading questions and the anxiety experienced at the time of the event had little or no effect on their subsequent memory of the event. These results refute the weapon focus effect and show that in real-life cases of extreme anxiety, the accuracy of eyewitness testimony is not affected.

Effective use of a real-life case study, in comparison with laboratory-based research, creates a well-elaborated argument.

Loftus' (Johnson and Scott's) research has been criticised for lacking ecological validity. Although the participants were waiting in the reception area outside the laboratory, they may have anticipated that something was going to happen, which could have affected the accuracy of their judgements. Furthermore, the results from real-life case studies (e.g. Yuille and Cutshall) refute the findings of Loftus and suggest that her results do not represent real-life cases of extreme anxiety.

Methodological critiques of the validity of the research furthers the discussion.

A final criticism of this research is that numerous ethical guidelines were broken. The participants were deceived about the nature of the experiment and not protected from harm. Loftus (Johnson and Scott) exposed some of the participants to a man holding a bloodied knife, which could have caused extreme feelings of anxiety. This is an issue, as these participants may have left the experiment feeling exceptionally stressed and anxious, especially if they, or someone they knew, had been involved in a knife crime.

Finally, an interesting ethical issue is raised for consideration.

Examiner style comments: *Mark band 4*

This is a well-detailed and accurate account of how anxiety can affect the recall and accuracy of eyewitness testimony, referring to a key piece of research in this area of psychology conducted by Johnson and Scott as reported by Loftus. The evaluation is thorough and effective in most places, and the final paragraph provides an interesting discussion of the ethical implications of conducting such research.

Discuss the use of the cognitive interview as a means of improving the accuracy of eyewitness testimony. (16 marks)

Geiselman *et al.* (1985) developed the cognitive interview, identifying four key principles that they believed would enhance recall of eyewitness testimony, compared to the standard police interview, including: context reinstatement (CR), report everything (RE), recall from a changed perspective (CP) and recall in reverse order (RO).

CR is when a person mentally recalls the context of the event, for example, the time of day and the weather. These details act as a trigger, helping the person recall more information. RE is when a person recalls every detail they can remember, even those that seem trivial. CP is when a person considers the event from someone else's point of view, for example, the offender. Finally, RO is where a person recalls the events in reverse chronological order.

Geiselman (1985) examined the effectiveness of the cognitive interview using students who watched a video of a simulated crime. Two days later, participants were interviewed using the standard police interview or the cognitive interview. Those who were interviewed using the cognitive interview recalled significantly more correct information than those interviewed using the standard interview. This suggests that the cognitive interview is more effective than a standard interview at eliciting information from eyewitnesses.

Fisher *et al.* (1989) support the results of Geiselman and therefore the effectiveness of the cognitive interview. These researchers examined the effectiveness of the cognitive interview in real police interviews. Experienced detectives recorded a selection of their interviews, using a standard interviewing technique. The detectives were then divided into two groups. One group was trained to use the cognitive interview, while the other group continued using the standard interview. After training, their subsequent interviews were analysed. The trained detectives elicited 46% more information after their training, in comparison to the control group. Where it was possible to confirm the information, over 90% of it was found to be accurate, thus providing further evidence for the cognitive interview as a technique to elicit more information which is highly accurate.

Although the cognitive interview increases the quantity of information recalled, research suggests that it is still susceptible to misleading information. Centofanti and Reece (2006) showed participants a video of a bank robbery and then provided participants with a misleading or neutral post-event summary. On average, the participants who were questioned using a cognitive interview recalled 35% more information. However, the participants in both conditions were equally susceptible to misleading information. Therefore, although the cognitive interview enhances the quantity of information recalled, interviewers need to be careful that participants are not exposed to misleading information.

Although research supports the effectiveness of the cognitive interview, Kebbell and Wagstaff (1996) have found that police typically use interviewing techniques that limit the quantity of information provided, rather than those that improve accuracy. Furthermore, the cognitive interview requires special training, and many police forces have not provided more than rudimentary training, which explains why the cognitive interview is not readily used. Therefore, despite the encouraging results found in relation to the cognitive interview, both in terms of helping witnesses to recall information and ensuring accuracy, the technique is not widely used due to the constraints placed on the police. Therefore, further research is required to devise a technique that the police could implement successfully.

A swift start to the essay outlining the main strategies involved in the cognitive interview.

Each strategy is outlined well with examples where appropriate.

Relevant research study used to enhance the description and provide some initial commentary.

Excellent choice of research to support the argument providing a good level of detail.

A counter-argument is provided to balance the evaluative commentary with both strengths and weaknesses of the cognitive interview.

An interesting problem associated with the limitations of using the cognitive interview in everyday police practice.

Examiner style comments: *Mark band 4*

This essay demonstrates an exceptionally clear understanding of the cognitive interview and its role in improving accuracy of eyewitness testimony. The outline knowledge is accurate and detailed, striking a balance between each strategy involved in the procedure in equal depth. The evaluation commentary is thorough, effective and focused on the demands of the question. The evaluation draws on suitable research evidence to provide an interesting discussion.

MEMORY KEY TERMS

Key term	Definition
Memory	A topic in psychology which examines how humans process and store information, the factors that affect the accuracy and reliability of eyewitness testimony, and how information is lost/forgotten.
Anxiety	Anxiety is a factor that has been shown to affect the accuracy of eyewitness testimony. Loftus proposed the 'weapon focus effect', which suggests that anxiety, caused by witnessing a weapon e.g. knife/gun, focuses attention away from details of the potential perpetrators and thus reduces the accuracy of eyewitness testimony.
Capacity	Capacity refers to the amount, or quantity, of information that can be stored in memory.
Central Executive	The central executive is the 'boss' of the WMM. It controls attention and directs information to the two slave systems: the phonological loop and visuospatial sketchpad. The central executive can process information from any sensory modality.
Coding	Coding refers to how information is changed and stored in memory.
Cognitive Interview	Geiselman *et al.* (1985) developed the cognitive interview in response to criticisms of the traditional police interview. Geiselman identified four key principles that he believed would enhance recall, including Context reinstatement (CR), Report everything (RE), Recall from changed perspective (CP) and Recall in reverse order (RO).
Duration	Duration refers to the length of time information is held in memory.
Episodic Memory	Episodic memory is a type of explicit memory which includes memories of personal experiences (episodes), such as your first day at school or when you last visited the doctor. These memories are more complex than you might realise and have three specific elements: details of the event, the context, and associated emotions, which are all interwoven to provide a single memory. The strength of episodic memories is determined by the strength of the emotions experienced when the memory is coded, and a conscious effort is required to retrieve them. Episodic memories are associated with the hippocampus.
Episodic Buffer	The episodic buffer is a part of the working memory model (WMM) which binds and integrates information from all the components and passes the information to long-term memory (LTM). It therefore codes both visual and acoustic information but does have a limited capacity.
Eyewitness Testimony	An eyewitness testimony is the evidence given in court or a police investigation by someone who has witnessed a crime or accident. For many years psychologists have investigated the factors that can affect the accuracy of eyewitness reports to ensure that the evidence provided during investigations is reliable and accurate. Psychologists have identified several factors that can have a detrimental effect on the accuracy of eyewitness reports, including misleading information which may result from leading questions or post-event discussion and anxiety.
Forgetting	Long-term memories are not always remembered, and forgetting can occur for different reasons. Psychologists have suggested different explanations for forgetting: proactive interference, retroactive interference and retrieval failure due to the absence of cues.
Leading Questions	Leading questions are those that are worded to suggest a particular answer. For example, 'Did you see the broken glass?' implies that there was broken glass and therefore a witness is more likely to say 'yes'.
Long-Term Memory	Long-term memory (LTM) is a 'permanent' store that holds unlimited amounts of information for long periods. There are different types of LTM: episodic, semantic and procedural.
Misleading Information	Misleading information is a key factor affecting the accuracy of eyewitness testimony. Misleading information is incorrect information given to an eyewitness following an event. This can occur during post-event discussion or take the form of leading questions.

Key term	Definition
Multi-Store Model	Atkinson & Shiffrin (1968) proposed the Multi-Store Model (MSM) which suggests that memory is made up of three components: sensory register (SR), short-term memory (STM) and long-term memory (LTM). According to the model, memories are formed sequentially, and information passes from one component to the next, in a linear fashion. Each of the three components has a specific type of coding, capacity and duration.
Phonological Loop	The phonological loop is a temporary storage system for verbal information (held in a speech-based form) which has two components: the articulatory control process (the 'inner voice') and the phonological store (the 'inner ear'). The articulatory control process allows for the subvocal repetition of acoustic information, and the phonological store is a temporary, limited capacity storage space for coding acoustic information.
Post-Event Discussion	Post-event discussion, when witnesses discuss what they saw after an event, is a potential source of misleading information. This can then affect the accuracy of their accounts.
Proactive Interference	Proactive interference occurs when old information stored in long-term memory interferes with the learning of new information. An everyday example of proactive interference is when you try to remember a new mobile phone number and your memory of your old number disrupts your attempts to recall this new information.
Procedural Memory	Procedural memory is a type of implicit memory, which includes remembering how to perform certain tasks, actions or skills, such as swimming, reading and writing which have become 'automatic'. They are difficult to explain in words to someone else and are often acquired through repetition and practice, for example, when we learn to ride a bike or drive a car.
Retrieval Failure	Retrieval failure is an explanation for forgetting from long-term memory. It refers to difficulties in recall that are due to the absence of correct retrieval cues or triggers. There are two types of retrieval failure due to the absence of cues: 1) context-dependent failure, and 2) state-dependent failure. Context-dependent failure occurs when environmental cues are missing, and state-dependent failure occurs when an individual's emotional state is different when trying to recall information.
Retroactive Interference	Retroactive interference occurs when the learning of new information interferes with the recall of old information from LTM. For example, once you have learned your new mobile number, it is often very difficult to recall your old number.
Semantic Memory	Semantic memory is a type of explicit memory of knowledge, facts, concepts and meaning about the world around us. For example, knowing that London is the capital of England. Semantic memories often start as episodic memories, but they are not 'time-stamped' in the same way nor do they remain closely associated with an event.
Sensory Register	The sensory register is the store where information first enters memory through the senses. There are separate sensory registers for each sense: the iconic store codes visual information and the echoic store codes auditory information. Information only lasts for a moment unless attention is directed to that register, which then transfers the information to STM.
Short-Term Memory	Short-term memory (STM) is a temporary memory store that holds a limited amount of information for a short period. The STM has a limited capacity of 7+/-2 'chunks' of information and a limited duration of approximately 20 seconds. Information in our STM is coded in an acoustic format.
Visuospatial Sketchpad	The visuospatial sketchpad is a temporary storage system for visual and spatial information which also has two components, the inner scribe and the visual cache. The inner scribe deals with the manipulation of mental images and the visual cache has a limited capacity for coding visual and spatial information.
Working Memory Model	Baddeley & Hitch (1974) put forward the working memory model (WMM) to explain some of the research findings that could not be explained by the MSM. The WMM is a multi-component, short-term memory system that consists of a central executive, phonological loop and visuospatial sketchpad.

NOTES

For more help and support in AQA A-Level
Psychology scan the QR code above.

www.tutor2u.net/psychology

AQA | A Level | Psychology

SKU: 03-4130-30098-03 | ISBN: 978-1915417176

X001J76EZB

AQA A-Level Psycholo... A-Level Psychology)
New

INTRODUCTION TO MEMORY

Memory is one of the compulsory topics on your AQA A-Level Psychology Paper 1.

For this topic, you should ensure that you are able to demonstrate your knowledge of theories, concepts, and studies as dictated by the specification. You should also be able to demonstate critical thinking, such as the strengths and limitations of memory models, and much more.

This booklet covers the memory topic in detail, and includes practice questions for you to attempt and assess your learning. A key term glossary and a selection of exemplar essays are included at the back.

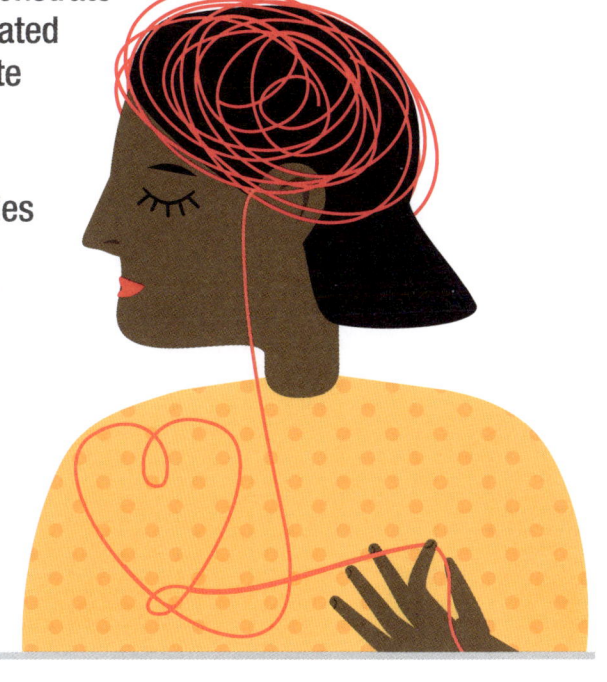

CONTENTS

CHAPTER 1	THE MULTI-STORE MODEL	Page 03
CHAPTER 2	TYPES OF LONG-TERM MEMORY	Page 08
CHAPTER 3	THE WORKING MEMORY MODEL	Page 11
CHAPTER 4	EXPLANATIONS FOR FORGETTING	Page 15
CHAPTER 5	EYEWITNESS TESTIMONY	Page 21
CHAPTER 6	IMPROVING THE ACCURACY OF EYE WITNESS TESTIMONY	Page 27
	EXAM STYLE QUESTIONS ON MEMORY	Page 30
	MEMORY KEY TERMS	Page 40

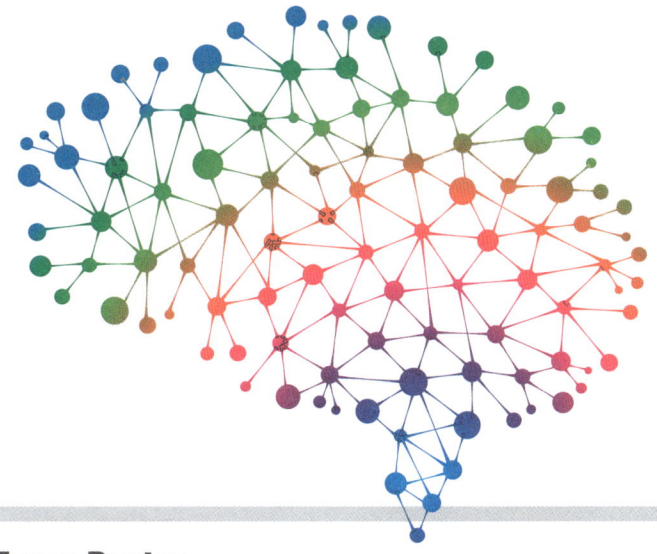

tutor2u

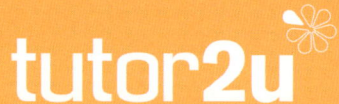

AQA A-LEVEL PSYCHOLOGY

MEMORY

EXAM BUSTER

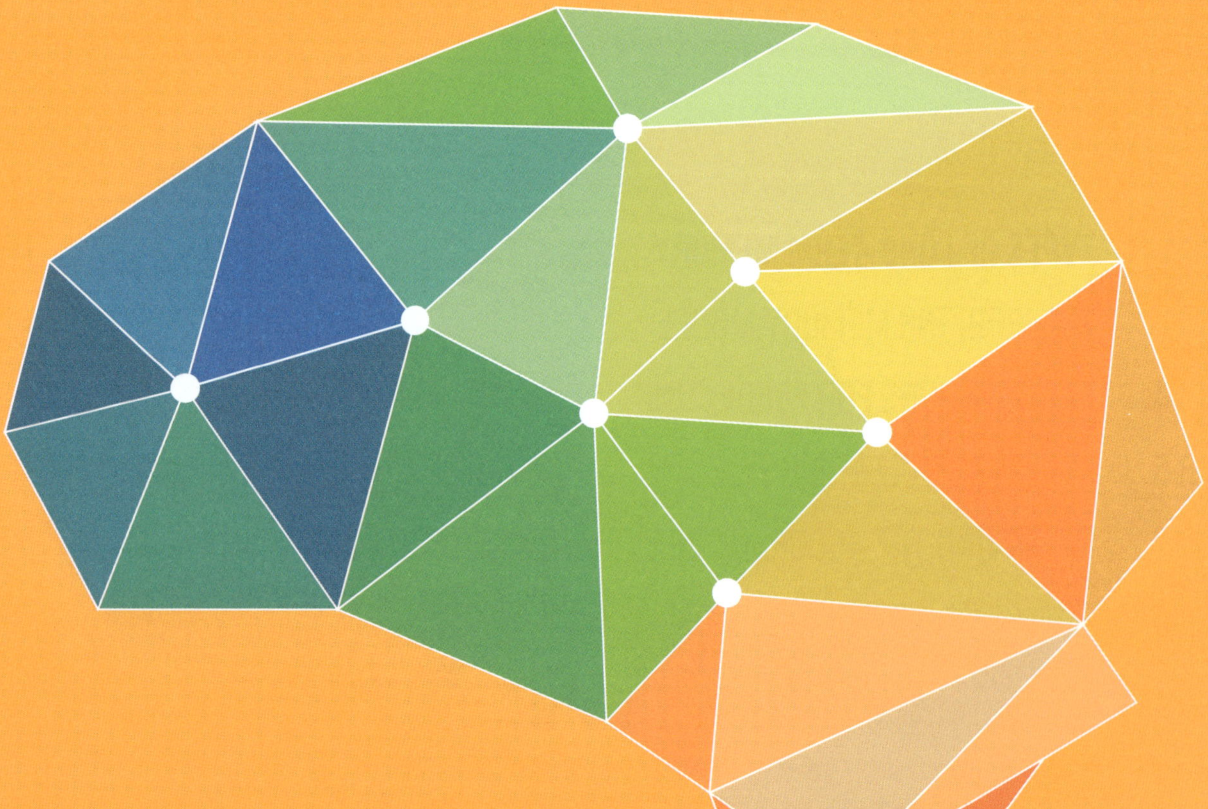

Student Name: